Bishop Rock Lighthouse

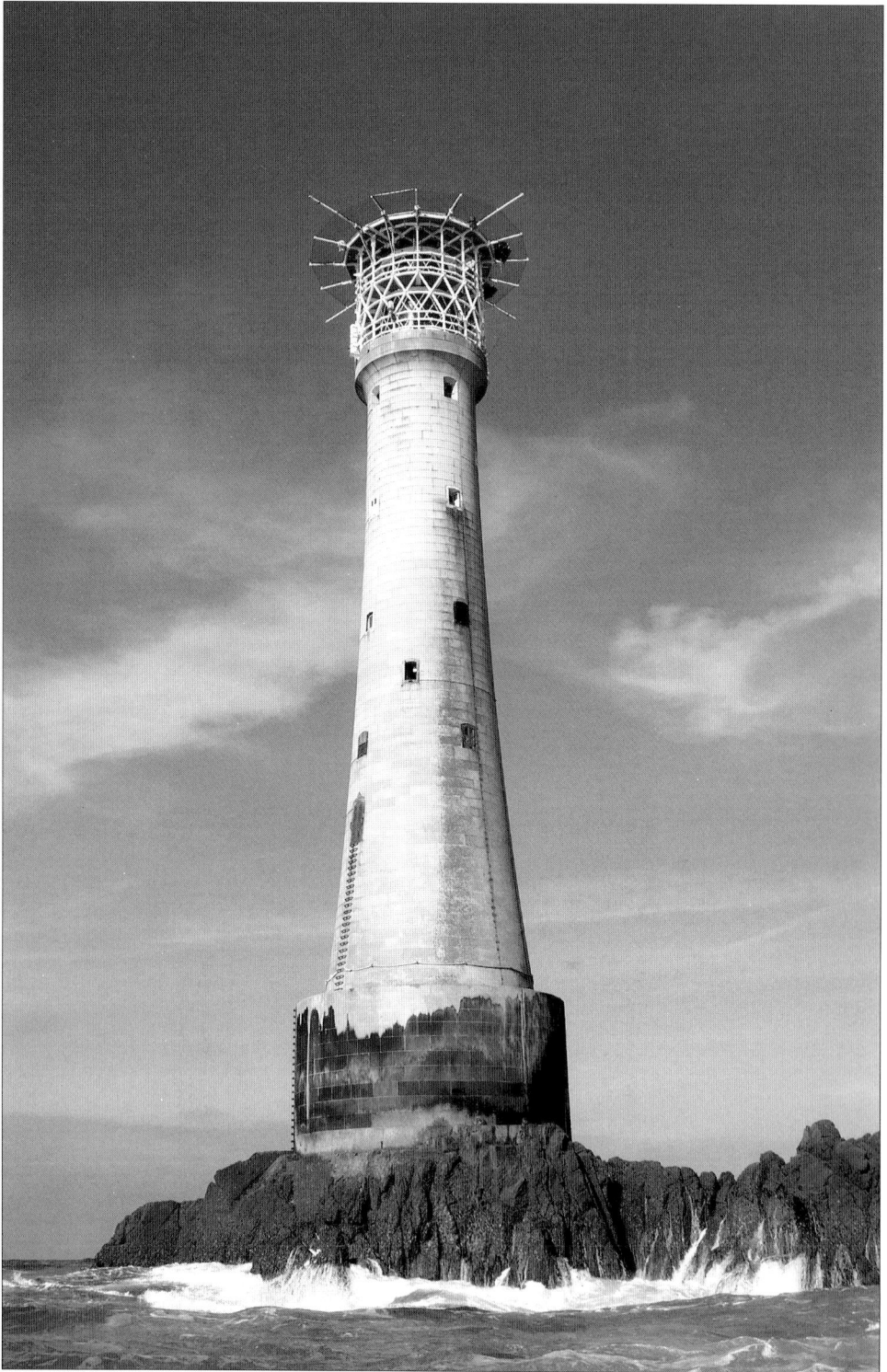

*Bishop Rock lighthouse.* ELISABETH STANBROOK

# Bishop Rock Lighthouse

*by*

Elisabeth Stanbrook

**TWELVEHEADS PRESS**

TRURO 2008

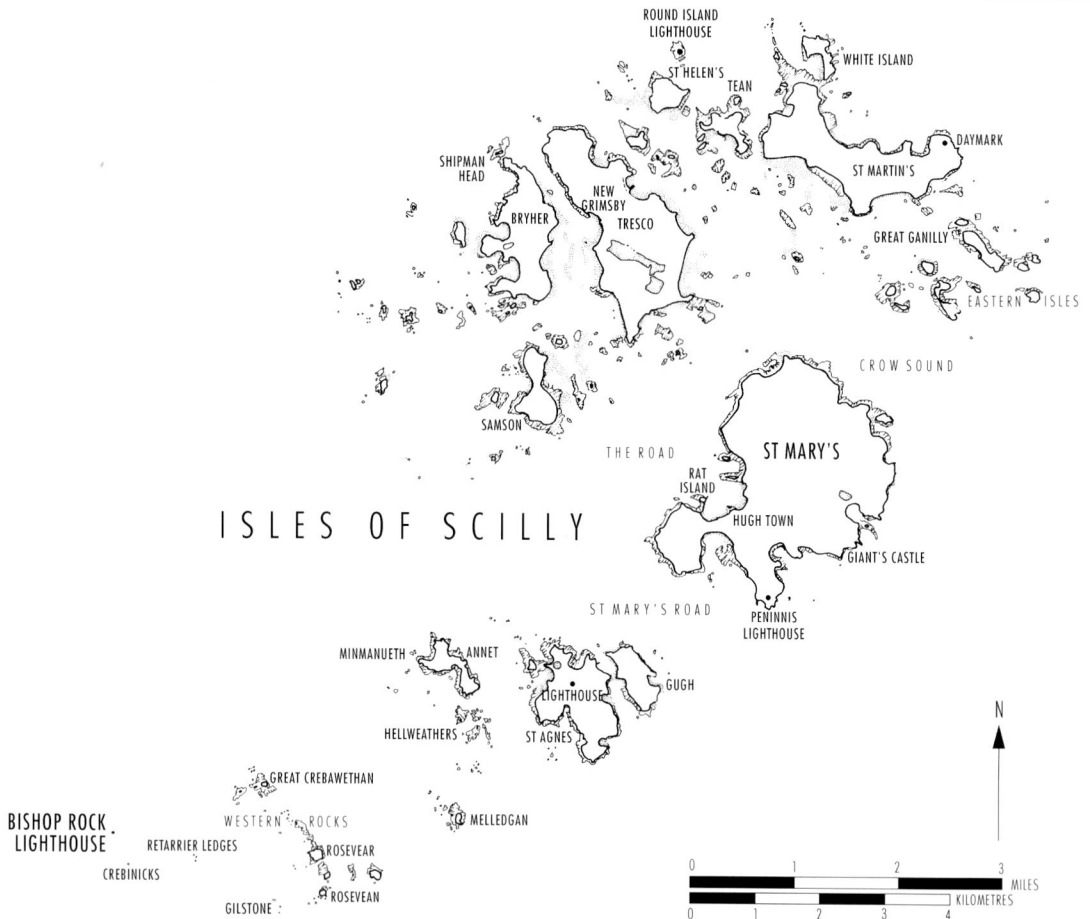

Map of the Isles of Scilly showing: ROUND ISLAND LIGHTHOUSE, ST HELEN'S, TEAN, WHITE ISLAND, DAYMARK, ST MARTIN'S, SHIPMAN HEAD, NEW GRIMSBY, BRYHER, TRESCO, GREAT GANILLY, EASTERN ISLES, CROW SOUND, SAMSON, THE ROAD, RAT ISLAND, ST MARY'S, HUGH TOWN, GIANT'S CASTLE, ST MARY'S ROAD, PENINNIS LIGHTHOUSE, MINMANUETH, ANNET, GUGH, LIGHTHOUSE, HELLWEATHERS, ST AGNES, GREAT CREBAWETHAN, WESTERN ROCKS, MELLEDGAN, BISHOP ROCK LIGHTHOUSE, RETARRIER LEDGES, ROSEVEAR, CREBINICKS, GILSTONE, ROSEVEAN. ISLES OF SCILLY.

Front cover, main picture: *Bishop Rock lighthouse.* ELISABETH STANBROOK
Front cover, inset pictures: *James Douglass.* INSTITUTION OF CIVIL ENGINEERS
*Principal Keeper John Ball.* STAN AND MARGRET BUTCHER (LIGHTHOUSE DUO)
*James Walker.* INSTITUTION OF CIVIL ENGINEERS
*A keeper at the light.* GIBSON ARCHIVE
Back cover: *Western Rocks.* ELISABETH STANBROOK
*The completed lighthouse in 1858.* ILLUSTRATED LONDON NEWS

**TWELVEHEADS PRESS**

First published 2008 by Twelveheads Press
ISBN 978 0 906294 69 7
British Library Cataloguing-in-Publication Data.
A catalogue record for this book is available from the British Library.
Printed by The Amadeus Press, Cleckheaton, West Yorkshire.

# Contents

*Looking towards Bishop Rock lighthouse.* ELISABETH STANBROOK

# Introduction

'When you survey the network of rocks which abound in these seas you will not wonder at the dread which so universally prevails, and the anxiety of all seamen to give Scilly a wide berth.'[1]

A mariner's dread when approaching the Isles of Scilly, which lie about 28 miles off Lands End, becomes perfectly understandable when one surveys the surrounding outcrops of granite, especially those of the dramatic Western Rocks off St Agnes. Bishop Rock is at the extreme western edge of these at grid reference SV 807064, latitude and longitude 49° 52' N, 6° 27' W.

A calm, sunny summer's day can make these rocks appear deceptively benign, but those witnessing a storm here know differently. With nothing between Scilly and America, they receive the full force of the Atlantic Ocean. Savage seas can rise up and crash down upon the rocky jagged teeth, menacing enough at low tide, but treacherous at high water when the jaws-in-waiting are partially hidden. Over the centuries, an indeterminable number of vessels have foundered here, and the seabed is a timeless graveyard of wrecks.

Probably the most famous wreck on Scilly is that of Sir Cloudesley Shovell's *Association*, together with his consort ships *Firebrand*, *Eagle* and *Romney* when, on 22 October 1707, an estimated fifteen hundred people died after they struck the Western Rocks, including the outer Gilstone. The sheer awfulness of this loss prompted the Longitude Act of 1714 with a prize of £20,000 offered to whoever could develop a means of working out longitude, so that seafarers could benefit from its use. It was clockmaker John Harrison who found the solution, but his fascinating story has been told elsewhere.[2] Other notable casualties off rocks around the Isles of Scilly were *Colossus* in 1798, *Schiller* in 1875 and *Thomas W. Lawson* in 1907, some with a very significant loss of life.

As the crow flies, Bishop Rock lies about 7 km (4 ½ miles) from the nearest part of the inhabited island of St Agnes, at Periglis, and 12 km (7 ½ miles) from St Mary's harbour. It comprises pink granite and rises to a height of about 45m from the seabed, is 46m long and 16m wide. It was

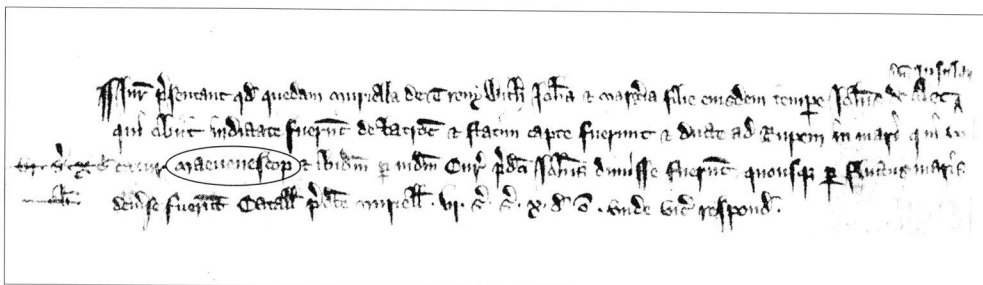

*1302 document showing a reference to Bishop Rock (maenenescop).* THE NATIONAL ARCHIVES

a prominent landmark to be seen by sailors when entering the English Channel, and became even more so when the lighthouse was built.

It is likely that Bishop Rock has always held great significance for those on the Isles of Scilly. Interestingly, but perhaps coincidentally, the chamber at Bants Carn, a prehistoric entrance grave on St Mary's, is aligned with Bishop Rock which, due to lower sea levels, would have stood higher by perhaps about 30 feet in prehistoric times. It is also possible that the rock was regarded as a special place, being the outermost boundary of Scilly.

There are various theories as to how Bishop Rock acquired its name, for example, its likeness to a bishop's mitre. In 1564 the 'byshop and hys clerkys' are mentioned,[3] while some say that in the 1660s, Miles Bishop together with John and Henry Clerk were wrecked in the *Royal Oake* on the rocks.[4] Charles Thomas records that in AD 384, two Spanish bishops, Instantius and Tiberianus, were found guilty of supporting the heresies of a layman called Priscillianus, and were exiled from Bordeaux to the Isles of Scilly as a punishment.[5] There may be some link with this event. Whatever, the rock's name actually long pre-dates the first reference to the Bishop and Clerks.

It was certainly of significance in medieval times when it is known to have been a place of execution as noted by Oliver Padel[6] and James Whetter.[7] Records dating from 1302[8] reveal a specific crime and punishment relating to women of Trenoweth, a farm at the north end of St Mary's:

> The jurors present that a certain Muriel de Trenywith and Joan and Margery her daughters in the time of John de Alet, lord of the island who died, were indicted of theft and were immediately taken and led to the rock in the sea which is called Maenenescop [ie. Bishop Rock] and there by the judgement of the court of the aforesaid John they were left until they were drowned by the tide. The chattels of the aforesaid Muriel come to 6s 10 1/2d for which the sheriff answers.

Another document dating to 1284[9], although not citing Bishop Rock by name, mentions criminals on Scilly being taken to a rock in the sea with a pitcher of water and a loaf of bread, and one can be confident that this was Bishop Rock. With such a grim history, did the fear and trauma, which must have been experienced on the rock, ever pervade the atmosphere of the lighthouse?

From at least medieval times onwards, there have been warning lights around the coast of Britain. Chapels, priories and ecclesiastical buildings on the coastline provided lights set in cressets or fire baskets. On the Isles of Scilly, records reveal that the chapel on Chapel Head (St Martin's Head), St Martin's was used as an ancient sea mark,[10] and a fire may have been lit here for night time navigation.

In 1514 Henry VIII issued a Royal Charter enabling a group of mariners, known as the Guild of the Holy Trinity, to regulate the pilotage of ships. These Elder Brethren comprised a Master, Wardens and Assistants, while the Younger Brethren formed the majority. They became known as the Corporation of Trinity House, and their headquarters were at Deptford on the River Thames. A few years later, in 1566, the Seamarks Act permitted Trinity House to establish a series of beacons in strategic places to aid shipping.

James I gave the Corporation the right to exercise the compulsory pilotage of shipping in 1604. According to Trinity House, their first two lighthouses were built at Lowestoft. These were rebuilt in 1628 and, in 1676, a replacement one was built higher up on a cliff.[11] The first lighthouse built on Scilly was on St Agnes in 1680.

From 1609 lighthouses became established all around the coast, many privately owned, and their owners could levy light dues on all passing ships when they entered ports. The quality of some of these lighthouses was questionable and eventually, in 1836, Trinity House was given the power to compulsorily purchase these and to maintain and manage them. Today, they maintain 69 lighthouses, both on isolated rocks and on the mainland.[12]

The number of shipwrecks around the Isles of Scilly will never be known, but thousands of people have perished in their treacherous waters. However, it is important to remember that both before and after the appearance of lighthouses on Scilly, many people have been saved too. The courage and tenacity of the local pilots and men in their gigs who went to their rescue in what were, often, terrible conditions should never be overlooked. And not all survived their heroic actions. Today, the Royal National Lifeboat Institution boat, stationed in St Mary's harbour, provides a magnificent service for seafarers caught out while at sea.

Key players in the early history of Bishop Rock lighthouse were the highly respected designers and engineers employed by Trinity House Corporation.

James Walker FRS, was Consultant Engineer to Trinity House, but he was also a dock and harbour engineer and head of his own private practice, Walker, Burges & Cooper. He designed both the original, ill-fated iron lighthouse, as well as the first granite tower completed in 1858. James Walker died in October 1862, just four years later.

Nicholas Douglass was head of a well known family of engineers. He was a Northumbrian man who had worked for the engineering firm Hunter & English. But, in 1839, he became a Construction Engineer for Trinity House, later becoming their Superintendent Engineer. It was he who invented bedding and side dovetailing masonry blocks. When these are set in Portland cement, they bond together with a strength similar to solid rock, and this was found to be an invaluable technique for building granite lighthouses. Nicholas died in 1881.

Nicholas's eldest son, James, was apprenticed to Hunter & English. He worked with his father on Bishop Rock lighthouse 1847-52 as Assistant Engineer, after which he left to work as Manager for R. J. & R. Laycock's railway carriage works at Stella in Newcastle-on-Tyne. He returned to Scilly in 1854 and married Mary Tregarthen, niece of Trinity House Agent, Hugh Tregarthen. He went back to Stella with his wife in 1855. In 1863, James became Engineer-in-Chief to Trinity House, upon the death of James Walker the previous year. He worked on lighthouses all over the world and, in June 1882, received a letter from the Prime Minister, Mr Gladstone, that Queen Victoria was to award him a knighthood for completing the Eddystone lighthouse, thought to be his most outstanding achievement. In October 1892, the Board of Trade sanctioned a retiring allowance of £1,200 p.a. to Sir James Douglass to take effect from 26 December 1892. Their approval and acknowledgement of his 'eminent services' was placed on record and communicated to him by letter. James died six years later in 1898.

James's younger brother William, also worked on the first granite tower and, when James left in 1852, he took over his brother's post. Between 1858 and 1862 he was Construction Engineer on the building of Les Hanois Rock lighthouse, Guernsey. Later, he became Engineer to the Commissioners of Irish Lights. He spent his retirement years in Penzance where he died in 1923.

William Tregarthen Douglass, James's son, followed in the footsteps of his father and grandfather and became Resident Engineer to Trinity House, working on the reconstruction of Bishop Rock lighthouse in the 1880s, and also the erection of Round Island lighthouse in 1887. When his father James retired, he was appointed Consulting Engineer to Trinity House. The Institution of Civil Engineers awarded the Telford Medal and a Telford Premium to William Tregarthen Douglass in 1892 for his account of 'The Bishop Rock Lighthouse' in their *Proceedings*. He died in

1913 after a boating accident off Start Point.

For some reason, Professor Michael Faraday is often omitted from accounts of Bishop Rock lighthouse, and yet his inventions were so important. He was a chemist and physicist who was interested in electromagnetism. He discovered the induction of electric currents and made the first dynamo. He worked as a laboratory assistant to Humphrey Davy, and succeeded him as Professor of Chemistry at the Royal Institution in 1833. Between 1836 and 1865 he was scientific advisor to Trinity House, and he explored the problem of condensation building up on the inside of a lighthouse's lantern due to lack of ventilation, causing the light to dim. He invented a type of chimney that carried this moisture to the outside of the lighthouse by means of a flue.

JAMES WALKER. PRESIDENT. 1835 TO 1845.

B.1781. PAINTED FOR THE MEMBERS OF THE INSTITUTION D.1862

*James Walker.*
INSTITUTION OF
CIVIL ENGINEERS

This book is not intended to be an in-depth technical discussion about the mechanical workings of Bishop Rock lighthouse, but rather a look at the story of one of Britain's most famous landmarks, how it came into being and its life to the present day. Primary sources, such as the Trinity House Board, Light and Wardens Committee minutes, plus other contemporary documents have revealed a compelling history. On occasion, I have digressed a little because I felt the information found might be of interest to some readers.

The saga starts in 1839 with the desperate need for a lighthouse on the Western Rocks under discussion by Trinity House, and traces the history through the various stages of development. After the abysmal failure of the iron structure, the decision to replace it with a granite one proved sound and, despite the need for a complete re-cladding in an outer coat of granite a couple of decades later, the lighthouse stands firm upon its rocky foundation still. The sometimes troubled provision of building materials, the accommodation for the workmen, the appalling weather conditions and the difficulties with communications, especially in the early days, are all discussed, as are the keepers themselves. Names have been identified

for the first ever four keepers to man the lighthouse. Details of keepers' lives at Bishop Rock have been touched upon, including misdemeanours, as has information about those men who operated the all-important relief boats.

Along the way there is much human interest, and a lot of information previously unpublished, including that about the lighthouse planned for Giants Castle Head on St Mary's. Dates and costings of work have been included where appropriate. At the end is an Appendix of known lighthouse keepers; names found either in the records or which were kindly supplied. This list is incomplete, both in terms of names and dates because, unfortunately, Trinity House does not hold details of every keeper, and I apologise for any omissions and inaccuracies that will have occurred. I would be delighted to learn of any additional information about keepers or the lighthouse in general.

Elisabeth Stanbrook

# CHAPTER ONE

# 1839 TO 1846

The terrifying ordeal of finding safe harbour in the waters of the Isles of Scilly during a storm, or navigating calmer waters in dense fog, must have been every mariner's dread. Even the lighthouse on St Agnes (1680) proved ineffective protection against the Western Rocks as it was obscured by various islands and landmarks. By the late 1830s, the possibility of placing a lighthouse on these rocks had been under discussion by Trinity House Corporation for several years. But it was in 1839, after the 140 ton brig *Theodorick*, en route from Mogadore, North West Africa to London, was wrecked on Bishop Rock, that concern over the number of wrecks in the area became paramount. One suggestion was that it should be built on the small islands of either Rosevean or Rosevear, while another was that one should also be built on St Martin's Head, the north-east part of the Scillonian archipelago.

## BISHOP ROCK IS CONSIDERED

Four years later the lighthouse had still not progressed beyond the planning stage, but Trinity House was now looking at Bishop Rock, which reportedly stood 15 feet above the sea (presumably at High Water), as the likely site. The year before, in October 1842, the steamer *Brigand*, carrying coal and fuel from Liverpool to London, also struck Bishop Rock. No crew perished, but the vessel and cargo were lost.

*Among the Western Rocks.*
ELISABETH
STANBROOK

It was in this year, too, that a survey of Bishop Rock and its dimensions had been undertaken by Mr Ellis, a pilot on Scilly. In February 1843 Trinity House decided that James Walker, their Consultant Engineer, would instruct Nicholas Douglass, their Superintendent Engineer, to take a break from his work on the Wolf Rock lighthouse and go and assess whether Bishop Rock was a stable and suitable site for a lighthouse. Here, they met with Trinity House Agent (and shipbuilder), Hugh Tregarthen, and they also inspected Rosevear and Rosevean at the same time. However, they all favoured Bishop Rock.

The results of his visit were presented to Trinity House in Walker's report of 2 June. Douglass had found that 13 feet would need to be taken off the rock to level it for foundations of 32 feet in diameter. He thought it to be a good rock on which to land materials, having deep water alongside, and estimated that 20 tons of stone could be landed per day in moderate weather.

There was another long time lapse, and serious discussion did not resume until January 1846, when it was considered prudent to install one of the best lights available at that time. This was, according to William Tregarthen Douglass writing in 1892,[1] considered to be 'an illuminating apparatus of the first order of "Fresnel" for a fixed light, having as its focus a 4-wick "Fresnel" burner consuming colza oil [a type of rapeseed oil], and giving an intensity in the beam of about 6,500 standard candles, with a nautical range of 15 $\frac{1}{2}$ miles'. In 1822 Augustin Fresnel had invented a lens comprising a convex lens and several prisms which focussed the light into an intense beam. This formed part of the illuminating apparatus.

At the same time, a fog bell weighing five hundredweight, was decided upon. This was to prove woefully inadequate.

GRANITE OR IRON?

A decision now had to be made as to whether to construct a granite or iron lighthouse on the rock. Smeaton's stone-built lighthouse on the Eddystone (1759), 13 miles south west of Plymouth, had been a success, while the survival of the first iron and timber lighthouse at the Smalls (1775), off the Pembrokeshire coast, was somewhat short-lived. But the development of ironworks during the early nineteenth century in south Wales led to other, longer lasting, ones being constructed entirely from cast iron around the Welsh coast and further afield.

Any building work undertaken on Bishop Rock meant that it would be a largely fair-weather project of a few months' duration each year, so a granite structure would ensure local employment preparing stones on shore during the winter months. Granite could be quarried on St Agnes as it was of good quality. Then, when finished, the lighthouse would be painted red.

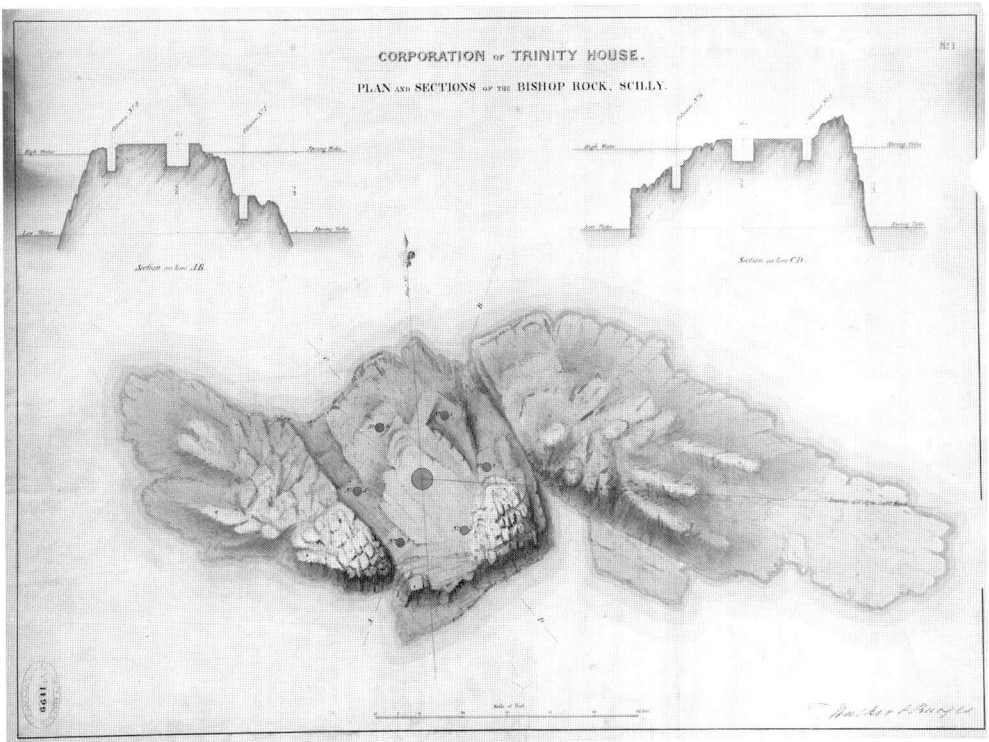

However, James Walker had become closely associated with Alexander Mitchell who, in the 1830s, had patented iron screwpile methods of constructing lighthouses. Mitchell had been contracted by Walker to fix piles on lighthouses of his design, such as those at Wyre near Fleetwood, Lancashire (1840) and Maplin (1841) off Foulness Island in the Thames Estuary on the south-eastern coast. These had been successful, showing no sign of weakness and able to withstand the sea, certainly in those more sheltered areas.

This association between the two men may have been instrumental in Walker's ill-fated decision to erect an iron screwpile lighthouse on Bishop Rock. He felt such a structure would allow waves to dissipate as they passed through the piles, rather than crashing against a solid building, and would therefore be more robust. Materials would not cost more than £3,000. Walker then proposed that Nicholas Douglass should be employed for the two seasons of work he thought would be necessary.

*Plan and sections of Bishop Rock.* TRINITY HOUSE

### ROSEVEAR AND THE BARRACKS

A plan was drawn up of a timber-built works depot and barracks to be erected on Rosevear* in which Douglass and the workmen would be accommodated while working on the lighthouse.

*Contemporary drawing of buildings on Rosevear by Sophia Tower.* COURTESY ROBERT DORRIEN SMITH AND SAM LLEWELLYN

Rosevear is a very roughly square, rocky island of about 5½ acres (2.17 hectares) in extent, or a maximum of about 220 yards x 220 yards (200m x 200m) at mean high water. It is 47 feet (14.3m) above sea level at its highest point. At two miles from Bishop Rock, it was the nearest island best suited for accommodation purposes, due to it having a small flat plateau. (See also map on p.33).

In mid-April 1846 members of the Light Committee left Plymouth in the Trinity House yacht, with a large boat in tow, for St Mary's. They called in at Penzance to collect Nicholas Douglass and nine workmen, who were to prepare Bishop Rock for building the lighthouse, and arrived at the Isles of Scilly that evening.

The following day the weather was good, and materials for building the barracks and stores were landed on Rosevear. What these workmen must have felt upon seeing the barrenness and remoteness of the island is not recorded, but at least some must have been rather taken aback knowing they were to be at the mercy of the elements should the weather turn suddenly. They set to work building their new quarters and, by 6pm that evening, the framework of the barracks had been finished. Construction was not far enough advanced to give them overnight shelter so, thankfully one might feel, they sailed back to St Mary's.

At about the same time, the buoys, chains and sinkers for Bishop Rock were delivered to Hugh Tregarthen on Tresco.

On the following Monday, Nicholas Douglass and his workmen

landed on Rosevear again, together with their clothes and bedding and a few remaining stores. The barracks were made habitable that day, and they were able to remain there.

In June the Light Committee returned to the Isles of Scilly and were taken out to Rosevear in a pilot boat which had on board Scillonian Nicholas Woodcock who was hoping to train to become a pilot. All seemed to be progressing well.

The *Exeter Flying Post* of 9 July 1846 incorrectly reported the lighthouse was to be erected on Rosevear, but there must have been some confusion with the barracks. They also reported that, after completion of the lighthouse, the one on St Agnes was to be raised 30 feet so that it could be seen more easily.

---

\* It has been suggested[2] that buildings were put up on Rosevear in the early eighteenth century as a base for Edmund Herbert's expedition in 1709-10 to salvage the wreck of the *Association*. This had come to grief in October 1707, when Sir Cloudesley Shovell and about fifteen hundred men perished in their fleet of ships. Although a base cannot be ruled out categorically, research for this book uncovered no evidence in the records of either Trinity House or personal papers of Edmund Herbert (now in a USA library), that any structures had been erected on the island before the 1840s. Herbert's accounts, which were fairly meticulous, and even included a reference to his dog's arrival on Scilly, do not mention any materials purchased to erect buildings or for taking them out to Rosevear. Indeed, Herbert himself stayed on St Mary's and hired boats to take him to such places as the Gilstone on 25 October 1709 (where he and five men retrieved a buckle) and Minalto on 29 October (when he and five men dived for ivory). Many other items were found during this expedition. Interestingly, on 26 August 1709 the diving engine used had been tested at 'Fox Hall' (presumably Vauxhall?) in London, in 3 ¹/₂ fathoms of water.

The suggestion of Herbert's base (which seems to have arisen in the last few decades of the twentieth century) may have been influenced by the find of a bronze cannon, thought to be from the *Association*, close to the island. This is now housed at the Valhalla Museum in Tresco Abbey Gardens.

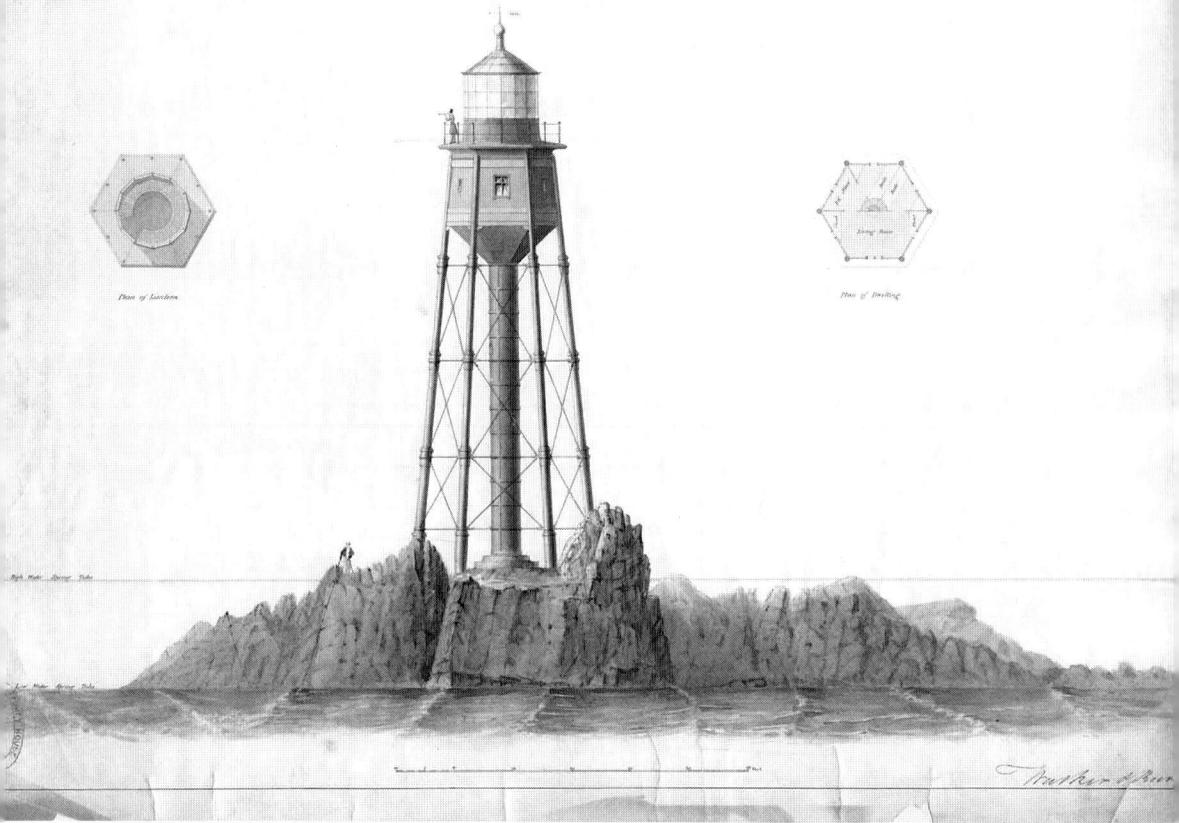

*Elevation of iron lighthouse.* TRINITY HOUSE

CHAPTER TWO

# 1847 TO FEBRUARY 1850

SPECIFICATIONS FOR THE LIGHTHOUSE

James Walker showed Trinity House his plan for the proposed iron screw-pile lighthouse in late March 1847. It was to be hexagonal, within a 40 feet diameter (as opposed to an initial plan of 35 feet), so that a height of 100 feet could be reached. He had made alterations to make it more stable by increasing the base, reducing the upper part of the lantern and dwelling, and increasing the diameter of the central cylinder from three to four feet so that access to the dwelling area was larger. The 35 feet long iron columns were to be strengthened by wrought-iron cores to be deeply entrenched into the rock.

The Committee ordered Walker to prepare specifications, which should then be given to C. Robinson & Son of Pimlico for an estimate of the weights, and prices for the cast and wrought iron required for the work.

His specifications for the lighthouse were:

Hexagonal, with a centre column 3 feet 6 inches in diameter, parallel from bottom upwards; and the outside columns 2 feet 1 inch diameter at bottom, tapering upwards to $10^{1/2}$ inches at top.

The middle column to be cast in lengths of about 7 feet with internal flanges and bolts to be in proportion to the strength of the cylinder, joggles to be cast on every other length of cylinder, to receive ends of stay-bars; a door to be fitted into the bottom length of Column, but its position cannot be specified until the Rock is inspected, and a ladder to be fitted to the inside of the column 14 inches wide; sides $2^{1/2}$ inches by $^{5/8}$ inches; the steps $^{7/8}$ inches diameter, and 9 inches distant.

Outside Columns: To be cast in 18 feet lengths stepping into each other 4 feet; the first length to be 2 feet 1 inch diameter outside, with a socket on top 4 feet deep and 2 feet 5 inches diameter fitted with a wrought iron hoop 5 inches by $2^{1/2}$ inches and rounded on the outside. The second length to be 2 feet diameter; socket 4 feet deep 2 feet $1^{1/2}$ inches diameter, and hoop

4 $\frac{1}{3}$ inches by 2 $\frac{1}{2}$. The third length to be 20 $\frac{1}{2}$ inches diameter; socket 4 inches deep 22 inches diameter; and hoop 4 $\frac{1}{3}$ inches by 2 $\frac{1}{2}$ inches. The fourth length to be 17 inches diameter; socket 4 feet deep 18 $\frac{1}{2}$ inches diameter; and hoop 4 inches by 2 $\frac{1}{2}$ inches. The fifth length to be 13 $\frac{1}{2}$ inches diameter; socket 4 feet deep 15 $\frac{1}{2}$ inches diameter, and hoop 3 $\frac{1}{2}$ inches by 2 $\frac{1}{3}$. The sixth length to be 10 inches diameter; socket 5 feet deep 12 $\frac{1}{3}$ inches diameter, and hoop 3 $\frac{1}{2}$ by 2 $\frac{1}{3}$ inches. The top length to be of wrought iron 33 feet long: diameter at top of socket 7 inches and 4 $\frac{1}{2}$ inches at the top end.

The six Outside Columns to be 1 $\frac{3}{4}$ inches thick. The Centre Column first two lengths to be 1 $\frac{3}{4}$ inches thick; third and fourth 1 $\frac{1}{2}$ inch; fifth and sixth 1 $\frac{1}{4}$ inch; all others upwards 1 inch thick.

The Outside Columns to have joggles cast on to receive dovetailed ends of horizontal Stay-bars; and each Socket to be filled with four sets of screws at bottom, and four keys at top.

First and Second Set of horizontal and diagonal Stay-bars to be 3 $\frac{1}{2}$ inches diameter, Third and Fourth Sets to be 3 inches diameter; and Fifth Set to be 2 $\frac{1}{2}$ inches diameter: the horizontal bars to form a dovetail at each end; and to be accurately fitted into joggles on column; to be secured with 1 $\frac{1}{2}$ inch bolt at each end; the diagonal stays to be fitted into joggles and secured with two 1 $\frac{1}{2}$ inch bolts at each end and one key. All castings to be of strong Gray Iron, Wrought Iron pillars to be best scrap iron and Stay-bars, bolts etc to be best 'S.C.' Iron.[1]

Walker obtained from C. Robinson & Son an acceptable estimate for the iron work in one total sum, which was £4,989 17s.

## AUGUSTUS SMITH

It is here that Augustus Smith, Lord Proprietor of the Isles of Scilly, comes onto the scene. He had leased Scilly from the Duchy of Cornwall in 1834 so, as lessee, his permission was sought for the works. It has been suggested that he advised against the iron structure which he felt was doomed.[2]

Although a certain degree of antagonism between Trinity House and Augustus Smith has been well documented in books, at this stage Smith does appear to have been amiable enough towards them. Writing from his home at Tresco Abbey on 15 April 1847, Smith informed Trinity House that he had never exercised any rights of property on Bishop Rock, so they could take possession of it without hindrance from him. He further consented to their occupying Rosevear for as long as they needed it, but asked that the people on the island 'may be charged not to molest in any way either the Sea fowl or their Nests on that or the adjoining Rocks and Islets'.[3] Their habitation of the island would coincide with the bird nesting season. Smith also wanted to arrange, with permission of the Duchy of Cornwall, accommodation for the future lighthouse keepers of Bishop Rock lighthouse, no doubt with their rent in mind. He was later to change his mind, as seen below.

Trinity House also wrote to the Duchy of Cornwall for permission to erect a lighthouse on Bishop Rock, and their response was favourable, wishing them well in the enterprise.

The pier on St Mary's had been extended during 1836-9 by Augustus Smith. This extension had incorporated Rat Island, which Trinity House saw as an ideal place for the workshops needed for stone dressing and carpentry work. No site could have been nearer to the pier for the transportation of goods out to the Western Rocks, and so they agreed a rent for this purpose with Smith.

*Augustus Smith*
TOM GREEVES
COLLECTION

## PREPARATION OF BISHOP ROCK BEGINS

Between 24 and 30 May 1847, Nicholas Douglass managed to complete 'two tides' of work and, by 6 June, he had completed five tides of work. The nature of this work had been to remove the loose part of the rock and prepare it for the cutting of holes to take the iron columns.

Writing from Rosevear in July, Douglass said it was not possible to get more than 30 feet diameter for the base of the columns and he was losing time waiting for Trinity House's decision to agree to this. In the end, they decided to send Alfred Burges, James Walker's business partner, to Bishop Rock to see if the diameter could not be nearer the 40 feet as proposed. But, having inspected the rock for himself, Burges confirmed that a larger base than 30 feet could not be accommodated and so, as a consequence, Walker proposed the height of the tower should be now 80 feet. New drawings were then made based on this (but from subsequent plans, it appears that the original height of 100 feet was maintained).

By 19 August, Douglass reported from Rosevear that work was so far advanced on Bishop Rock that he would be ready for the castings, to be sent in a tender, in about two weeks if the weather stayed moderate.

The Light Committee paid another visit to Scilly and landed on Bishop Rock for half an hour on Tuesday 9 September. They found the upper part of the rock had been removed and the surface partially levelled within the circle. They examined all the positions of the holes for the piles, and were satisfied that a circle of greater diameter could not have been obtained. All six holes had been excavated to a depth of five feet but the centre one had only been marked out.

In the meantime, new dwellings for the St Agnes lighthouse keepers were being built on that island. When a rough sea prevented a landing on Bishop Rock, the workmen on Rosevear were sent to St Agnes instead, where they quarried and prepared stones for the houses. They may have been glad of this time on a larger inhabited island, away from the close proximity of the relentless sea, despite the hard manual work.

In September, Douglass went to Plymouth with three of his men in search of a suitable boat for landing the castings on Bishop Rock. In due course, Mr Ditcham, the Trinity House Superintendent at Plymouth, reported that Douglass had found a suitable four-year-old vessel called *Billow*, at 52 tons, and costing £430.

CONSTRUCTION BEGINS

On 11 February 1848 Burges and Walker reported that there would be some bottom plates and wrought iron work of about ten or 12 tons ready in two weeks for shipment. They were ordered to send these to the Trinity House Buoy Wharf, London for shipment to Scilly in the tender *Billow*.

Despite the ironwork being of great weight, this would not always save it from the strength of wave and wind power, which were to be of great hindrance to the workmen throughout the building work. Douglass reported[4] that when a particular iron column weighing three tons had been landed on Bishop Rock, the weather became too rough to erect it so its foot was lashed to the rock using eyebolts and $1/2$ inch chain, while the upper end was secured to the tower frame; thus it was secured vertically. Three days later, a trip around Bishop Rock by interested parties revealed that the column had been tossed up 20 feet on to the top of the rock, and was swaying about horizontally like a piece of timber, being held by the lashings at its upper end only. It was discovered, upon landing on the rock a few days later, that the blacksmith's anvil ($1 1/2$ hundredweight) had been washed out of a hole, three feet six inches deep and two feet in diameter, prepared for the column. This should have served as a warning of what was to come! After all, the pressure of waves against the rock could be as much as 7,000lb per square inch.[5]

Some idea of the working hours was documented. James Douglass, Nicholas's elder son, said the men had worked on Bishop Rock during one tide on 30 March and on 1 and 2 April 1848, while for the week ending 29 April, his father said the men had worked 38 1/2 hours. For the week ending 6 May, they had worked 21 hours, while in the week ending 27 May, the men had been employed 37 1/2 hours on the rock. These variations were caused by changing weather conditions and the tides. A spell of fine, calm weather must have been a huge relief to the workmen as it meant more building work could be achieved, and in safer conditions. Writing from Rosevear on 13 June, Nicholas Douglass asked Trinity House for another tier of castings to be supplied immediately. A few days later, he was able to report that he had made considerable progress in fixing the lower tier of castings, and that if the weather was favourable for another week, he would run out of castings and other items needed to continue.

But the weather turned. In July Douglass was compelled to report that, due to unfavourable weather, no work had been done on Bishop Rock since 19 July, by which time five of the lower tiers of the outside columns were in place, as were the pieces of the centre column. By 22 August, conditions had not improved and work remained at a standstill. But by the week ending 16 September, better weather meant the men had managed to work 50 1/2 hours.

Douglass said he would not need the tender at Bishop Rock for some time as he intended to go to Plymouth for a cargo of limestone, and to call at Penzance for slate for floors for the new dwellings at St Agnes.

Construction continued and, by 10 October, the fourth tier of the columns had been placed. But on 17 October, work for that season ceased, and Nicholas Douglass left Scilly altogether on 21 October.

February 1849 was an expensive month. N. Holman & Sons, a foundry in St Just, sent in a bill for £240 3s 7d for unspecified iron items for the lighthouse. Another £600 was paid to C. Robinson & Son, plus a further £730 at the end of the month. They had asked for £1,000 because the work was so far advanced, but to no avail. They also sent in an acceptable tender for a cylinder and materials required for the lighthouse - cast iron costing 13s a hundredweight and wrought iron costing 6d a lb. They also tendered for tools required by Douglass.

Before the next season's work started, Hugh Tregarthen sailed out to Bishop Rock to check that all was well, and was able to assure Trinity House that the pillars had survived the winter without mishap, seen as a deceptively good sign, no doubt. At the start of May, Nicholas Douglass requested the next tier of castings, together with various other items, be sent as soon as possible. James Walker's report in mid-May recommended that the doorway in the centre column of the lighthouse should be placed higher than originally intended.

## HEAVY SEAS CAUSE DAMAGE AND LOSS

It was not always the winter months that produced the destructive seas. On 24 May 1849 Douglass wrote from Rosevear saying that a very heavy sea during the previous week had resulted in the loss of one piece of the second tier of outside columns and two plates of the centre column, together with the 'Sheers and Gear', the former being 40 feet high. New castings had to be ordered to replace those lost, and these arrived the following month.

Douglass did manage, with great difficulty, to land on Bishop Rock during that week, and found that no shaking had occurred to the rest of the fixed ironwork. However, on a second visit not long afterwards, a closer inspection revealed further damage including a fracture to the bottom length of column No.4 which had been caused by the centre plates striking the stay bar. As a result, he ordered the casting of a socket in Penzance, which would be as strong as before.

Members of the Light Committee sailed out to the Isles of Scilly on Thursday 5 July with a heavy cargo of iron pillars and castings destined for Bishop Rock, and 16 tons of coal from the Cattewater, Plymouth. They landed the cargo over a period of several days and picked up an iron pillar sent by mistake by C. Robinson & Son.

Ironically, the building of a structure destined to prevent maritime disasters was causing just that. In early August, it became apparent that the half-built lighthouse was misleading some seafarers. Hugh Tregarthen reported wreckage being found on some of the islands, and that 'Several Masters of Vessels from the westward have mistaken the structure on Bishop Rock for a ship under canvas'.[6] Although no further information was given in the records, this obviously was a serious situation with bad consequences.

## LANTERN, LIGHTING AND JOINERY

All the pillars had been landed on Bishop Rock by September 1849, and Nicholas Douglass reported that they had got four of the top pieces of the columns in their places and they would be ready for a lantern at the end of that week if the weather was favourable. Consequently a lantern was ordered from Wilkins & Co of London, to be manufactured from gun metal for £1,554 3s 9d. It would not be ready for shipment before October or the beginning of November. The window for the keepers' living room would be wanted as soon as possible too.

James Walker sent Trinity House a plan for the fitting up of the dwelling and store room floors, showing window sashes and frames etc. He said that the whole of these were joiners work and no part should be fixed until the lantern was up and glazed. If necessary, the window openings could be battened up with rough boarding for the present. He then said that his recommendation that the entrance door be changed had not been done by Douglass.

In response to this report, Trinity House ordered Walker to get the joiners' work in hand so that it could be ready for conveyance to Scilly at the same time as the lantern. Inspecting his plans, they commented that much room was lost in the oil store by the cisterns being circular, which might be saved if they were made to fit in the most convenient part of the cellar. Also, and rather surprisingly, there seemed to be no provision for the stowage of a supply of water, for the weight of a revolving machine, or for a crane, all of which required attention.

As the lantern was not to be fitted that season, Douglass told Trinity House that he would only undertake work that was absolutely

*Contemporary drawing of the lighthouse in 1849 by Sophia Tower.* COURTESY ROBERT DORRIEN SMITH AND SAM LLEWELLYN

necessary. They did not like this stance. It was pointed out to Douglass that no such decision had been taken by them and that the lantern was to be fitted as soon as it was ready. They ordered Douglass to leave the scaffolding in place for such an occasion. And so the work continued.

It was during this season that Lady Sophia Tower, a close friend of Augustus Smith, went on an expedition around the Western Rocks and saw the nearly completed iron lighthouse. As an amateur artist, she sketched the structure which was to provide a good layman's record of its appearance in 1849.

On 22 September Douglass sent a report from Rosevear saying that if the weather stayed moderate for another week he hoped to finish all that was requisite at Bishop Rock for that season. He was still there on 15 October when he wrote saying that he had got the lighthouse's six diagonal stay bars fixed and that the boarding was ready to cover the house. His son and men would take the first favourable opportunity to go down and close it up for the season.

Thus, with the exception of the lantern and lighting apparatus, the lighthouse was finished at the close of 1849. The delay in acquiring and fitting these was to prove fortuitous.

*Artist's impression of the finished iron lighthouse in 1849.*
ILLUSTRATED LONDON NEWS

On 15 January 1850 the Light Committee ordered the lighting apparatus and recommended a flashing light of equal duration of light and darkness for the lighthouse. Mr Wilkins of Wilkins & Co advised that the apparatus should contain 24 sections with top and bottom zones complete. He was told to procure one from France, and a 4-wick Fresnel burner was ordered.

## DISASTER STRIKES

A lighthouse built on a place of execution could be seen as inauspicious. On 4 February 1850 a terrific and catastrophic storm hit the Isles of Scilly and raged for about three days. This was to prove the death knell for the iron lighthouse, an embarrassing failure which James Walker, together with Nicholas Douglass, had to bear. Hugh Tregarthen wrote to Trinity House advising them of the fall, at about 3am on 6 February, of Bishop Rock lighthouse while the wind was at its highest. Compelled to regard the scene from a distance, he was under the impression that the lighthouse had been entirely demolished by the sea as he could not see any pillars remaining above the rock. Nicholas Douglass, who was in London at the time, was ordered to go to Scilly immediately to see the damage for himself. However, he did not arrive there until 24 February.

In the meantime, reporting further on 16 February, Hugh Tregarthen said that due to bad weather he had only managed to get to Bishop Rock the day before. He was able to give a more encouraging report and Trinity House minutes record: 'The N.W. or longest lower pillar standing with the Stay Bar on its Top, apparently perfect, and he apprehended that some of the lower pillars may be standing; and that he does not believe that any portion of the Rock where the pillars were fix'd is gone'.[7]

But, on 1 March, Douglass sent a more gloomy account. He had found columns of the structure broken off, and gave the following details:

No. 1 Broken 6 feet from the face of the Rock
No. 2 Broken 2 feet, 6 inches from the face of the Rock
No. 3 Broken level with the Rock
No. 4 Broken 4 feet from the face of the Rock
No. 5 Broken 1 foot, 1 inch from the face of the Rock
No. 6 Broken 1 foot, 1 inch from the face of the Rock

The centre two plates were broken to the level of the rock, and one plate was uninjured. Fortunately, as indicated by Mr Tregarthen, the rock itself was not affected.

In recent years, divers have found part of one of the iron pillars on a ledge 27 metres below the surface, and various other bits of associated metalwork.[8]

Had the lighthouse been finished in 1849, it would have been manned by lighthouse keepers, with the consequential loss of life, so it was extremely fortunate that installation of the lantern had been delayed. On 9 February Walker wrote to this effect to Mr Jacob Herbert, Secretary to Trinity House.

Forty-two years later, William Tregarthen Douglass said the disaster was due to heavy seas sweeping over the rock at heights higher than had been anticipated. With their full force, they had struck the larger surface of the upper part of the lighthouse, being the keepers' quarters and storage space.[9]

In a discussion about this episode in 1891,[10] Sir James Douglass said he felt the loss of the iron lighthouse was fortuitous in that it provided them with a greater understanding of the power of the sea and wave action at Bishop Rock which he described as heavier than anything he had ever seen during his travels all over the world.

It would seem that all parties had underestimated the power of the sea, never having experienced its ferocity on such a scale before.

PROPOSED IRON LIGHTHOUSE SPECIFICATIONS
Height of tower: 100 feet (with plans to reduce it to 80 feet)
Height of proposed light above MHW: 94 feet
Light source: Fresnel 4-wick burner and lens
Character: Flashing light of equal duration of light and darkness
Candle power: 6,500
Range of light: 15$\frac{1}{2}$ nautical miles
Fog warning apparatus: Five hundredweight bell
Cost: £12,500

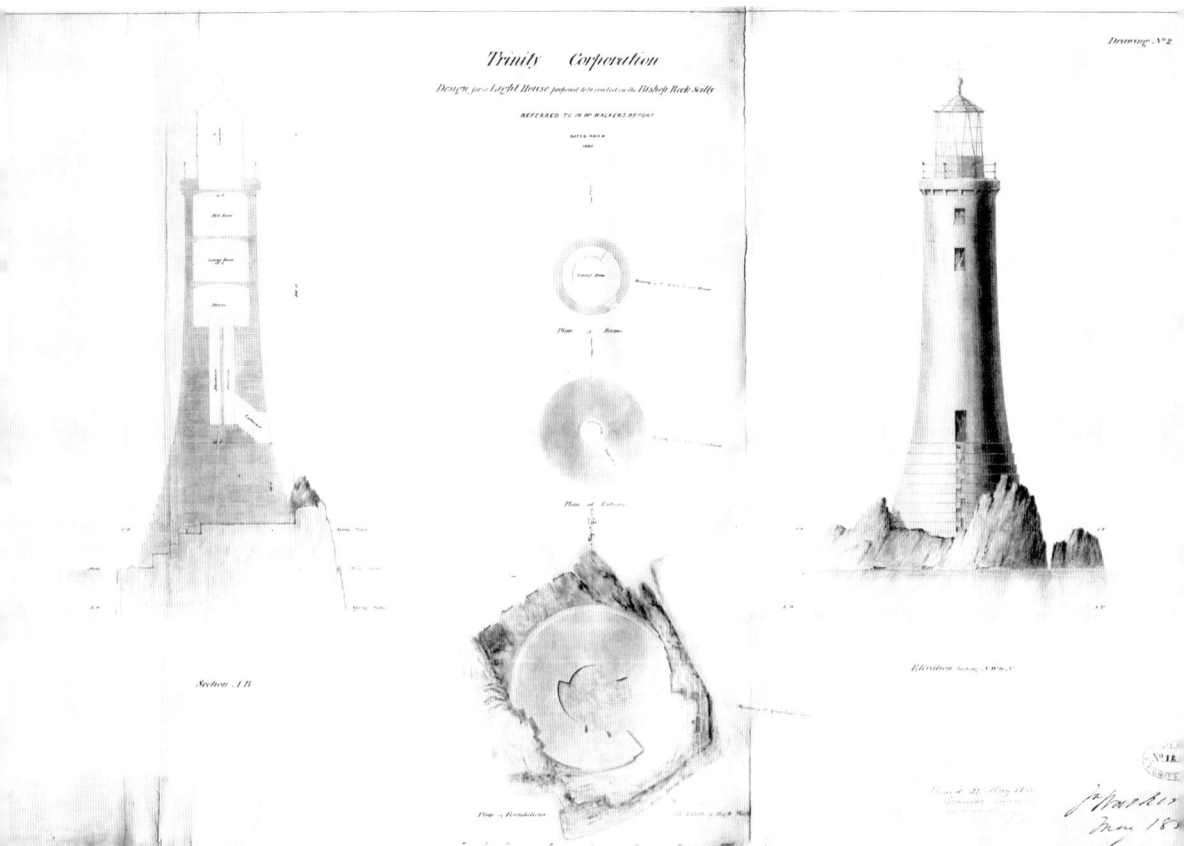

*Section, elevation and foundation plan of the first granite lighthouse in 1850.*
TRINITY HOUSE

# CHAPTER THREE

# 1850 TO 1858

Not surprisingly, the loss of Bishop Rock lighthouse made national news. This resulted in several would-be designers forwarding their plans for a replacement to Trinity House. For example, Capt W. S. Moorsom C.E. had 'insinuated his wish to be allowed to send in a plan for erecting a Light House on the said Rock', which he did.[1] But he later withdrew his offer. This was followed, in late May, by Mr William Burrall of Hayle Foundry in Cornwall proposing to submit drawings and specifications for a wrought iron lighthouse. Capt Samuel Brown, RN, wrote on 10 September 1850 proposing to erect one made with brass columns. Cornishman Samuel Moyle, a civil engineer, wrote from the Queen's Arms Hotel, London, on 1 February 1851, also wanting to erect a lighthouse. Other people were prompted to express the opinion that the lighthouse should have been built on Rosevear, including Mr William Mumford a member of a well known Scillonian family.

The lantern, no longer needed, was delivered to Blackwall during April, and there it remained, with no lighthouse on which to put it. Details of Wilkins's account on 17 September that year, showed that it stood at £2,271 12s 4d with a balance due to him of £471 12s 4d.

## ANOTHER ATTEMPT CONSIDERED

On 14 May 1850, despite the catastrophic failure of the iron structure, Trinity House considered James Walker's plan for building another lighthouse on Bishop Rock. Discussing this failure, Walker felt that the strength of the iron near the surface of the rock was insufficient to resist the might of the sea striking the iron at a higher level, resulting in a force of leverage. Although the iron lighthouse was incomplete, he felt the strength would have been much increased had the centre column been fitted up and strengthened to the proposed height and for which the materials were prepared. He was, nevertheless, reluctant to 'experiment' with another cast iron structure in that location, and who can blame him? The surface of the rock, in order to gain a larger base, would need to be lowered even further or raised up by stone to create a level surface to receive the iron. His main concern with the cast iron, especially the tubes, was its brittleness, the uncertainty as to the quality of the iron generally, the soundness of the castings when large, and the uniformity of thickness. Having examined pieces of iron broken off at the point of fracture of one of the columns, he concluded that some defects were caused in the casting by the foundry.[2]

Instead, Walker said wrought iron must be considered. He had discussed the matter with Hawks & Co of Newcastle, a firm which he considered one of the most experienced in the country for large forgings. On the basis of these discussions he came up with Plans 1 and 2 below.

But it was Plan 3, for a stone lighthouse, that Walker preferred, and was the one he had submitted to Trinity House in 1846. At low water it would be seen from a distance of 17.5 miles by a spectator raised 16 feet above the water; at high water this would be 16.5 miles. It was not dissimilar to other stone towers including those of Eddystone, Menai and Plymouth Breakwater.

In his report,[3] Walker gave the elevations from mean tide level to the centre of the lantern for various lighthouses, which provide interesting comparisons:

Menai ...............................................................72ft
Edystone [sic] ..................................................80ft
Smalls ..............................................................78ft
Iron plan B for the Bishop ..............................85ft
Bell Rock ........................................................99ft
Stone Tower now proposed for the Bishop........100ft
Skerryvore......................................................155ft

The stone tower proposed for Bishop Rock would contain 30,000 cubic feet of stone at £18,000; five seasons of work plus steam or other vessels to transport stone at £15,000; and £3,600 for unforeseen necessities.

In summary, James Walker's three proposals were:

1. By removing the Concrete and the remains of the Iron Pipes of the Structure recently destroy'd, and inserting in place thereof Wrought Iron Columns, of various lengths, corresponding with the level of the Rock, and raising thereon a Structure composed entirely of Malleable Iron; the Light thereon to be 80 feet above the Mean Level of the Sea: The total Cost of this Building he estimates at £22,500.

2. A modification of the foregoing, the Iron-Work being the Same, but in place of carrying the Pillars down to suit the inequalities of the Rock, by which the Legs are of unequal length, and therefore of unequal strength, the Rock is brought

On Rosevear in the
1890s.
GIBSON ARCHIVE

up to a level by courses of solid stone: In this building the Light would be 85 feet above the level of the Sea. This he considers would be the strongest Iron Structure, and he estimates the cost at £25,200.

3. A Granite Tower, being, in design, the same as that which he submitted in 1846, the diameter at bottom 33 feet, at the top under the cornice 17 feet, and the height to the Light from the Mean Sea Level 100 feet: The Cost of this Tower Mr Walker estimates at £36,000.

Walker now felt the stone tower preferable because of the danger during erection, and security afterwards. If Plans 1 and 2 were to be seriously considered, he preferred 2.

The shock of losing the cast iron lighthouse made Trinity House reflect upon the suitability of Bishop Rock for such a structure, but Walker was able to assure them he had no doubts at all as to its suitability. In putting their minds at rest, he described the rock thus: 'It is nearly upright on the North West side, but on that side only, and in all other directions either the length of the Rock or the slope of its sides, is considerable.'[4] So, after due consideration, Trinity House agreed to the building of a stone tower on the rock.

ROSEVEAR

On the morning of 27 June 1850 the workmen to be employed in the building of Bishop Rock lighthouse set sail for Scilly from Penzance. Again, Rosevear was used as a base, but granite buildings replaced those of timber.

These buildings are now completely ruinous, with just a few walls and gables surviving, bearing testimony to the men who lived and worked here under what must have been, at times, incredibly miserable and uncomfortable conditions.

Fortunately, the Ordnance Survey map (1:10,560 sheet 88NE and SE) surveyed in 1887 (revised 1906) gives a bird's eye view of the encampment and, together with recent archaeological surveys of the island, a good picture of what the complex comprised can be obtained. The buildings were erected on the only flat area of Rosevear, to the north-east and east. They were constructed from bedrock granite, cut by the feather and tare method from along the northern edge of the island, and from granite rubble.

The westernmost building (No.1 on the annotated map), had one large room measuring internally 5.5m long and 3.25m wide. The walls survive to a height of approximately 1.6m with a gable at each end, the eastern one being about three metres in height. The western gable incorporates a large bedrock boulder in which it is thought are holes for purlins. This suggests that the building had a roof space, maybe for storage or even sleeping accommodation. The western side of this building has an annexe extending 3.3m. There are two window openings on the north wall and a doorway on the south wall. There is a walled yard attached to the south side of the building, and roof slates can be found on the ground. This building may have been for accommodation, and is the building one sees today on a boat trip around the Western Rocks.

The walls of the north-eastern building (No.2 on the annotated map) survive to a height of about 1.4m, and large boulders are incorporated. It is divided into two compartments, the eastern one being 8.2m x 5.5m, while the western one is 3.3m x 2.75m. The remains of what may be a window can be found in the north wall while, in the south are the doorways which share an L-shaped porch. Archaeologists have concluded that this building may never have had a roof as the walls appear to have been capped with individual stones, so it may have formed workyards.

The southernmost building (No.3 on the annotated map) had a large opening onto the south-east seaward side and is thought to have been a possible boathouse.[5] Today nothing remains of it but a rubble spread, but in the 1890s a good photographic record was made by the Gibson family.

There is an apparent stone platform on the east side of the island, about 15m south-east of building No.3, which is very ruinous. It is rectangular, 3.2m wide, extending to 3.4m. One theory is that it was a loading platform or base for a small crane or derrick; another is that it is the collapsed wall of another building, although the feature is not shown on the 1887 map.

Another item examined by archaeologists is a large rounded hollow rock, naturally weathered and measuring 0.4m deep and 0.75m in diameter. Signs of intense heat have made it a possible candidate for a smithing hearth.

Archaeologists from the Cornwall Archaeological Unit also recorded the stump of a flagpole when visiting Rosevear in 1988.[6] Also, on the west of the island was a trigonometrical station. This, together with others on adjoining islands, is shown on the Ordnance Survey map sheet 88NE and SE.

*O.S. map of Rosevear in 1887.*

In his book *The Scilly Isles*, Grigson said that clinker could still be found on Rosevear, and that the buildings provide 'a typical piece of island vernacular, with the windows opening out at an angle, giving the maximum of light with the minimum of window space.'[7] Also surviving is a former slipway or quay with associated metalwork.[8] Writing in the 1950s, Wendy Aldridge commented on the trace of a rough quay, an aspect not generally mentioned by others.[9] The island is, today, covered in sea mallow and is a protected site.

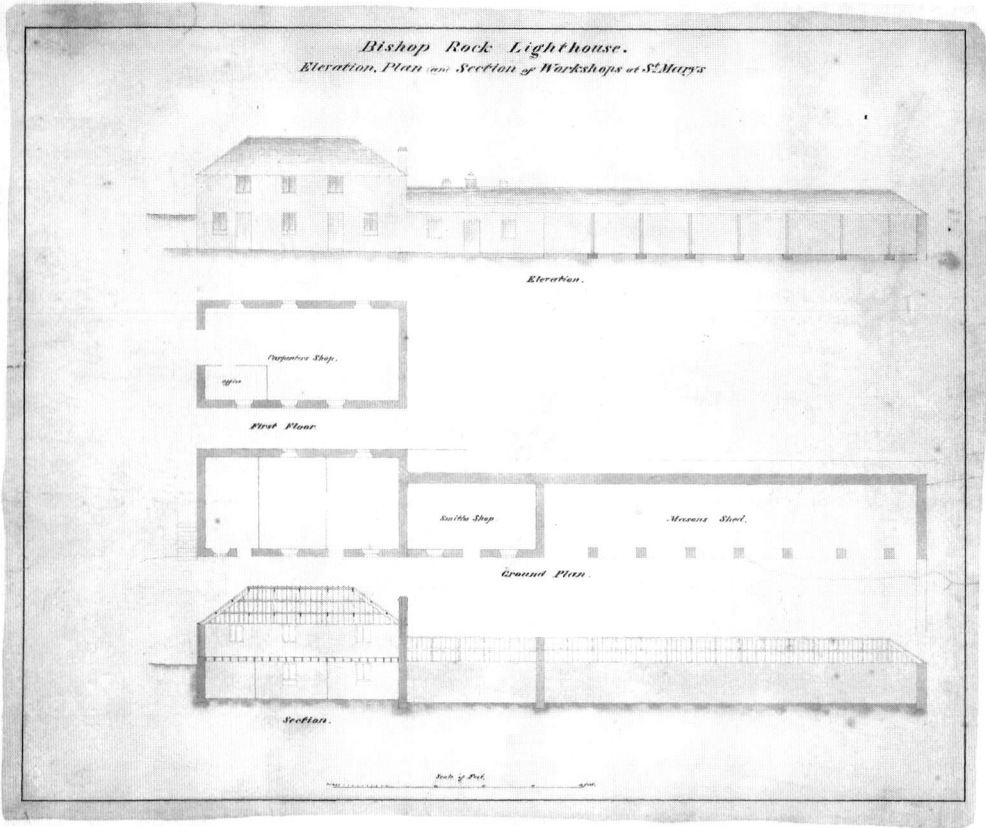

Bishop Rock Lighthouse.
Elevation, Plan and Section of Workshops at St Mary's

*Plan of the workshops on Rat Island, St Mary's.* TRINITY HOUSE

PREPARATION WORK BEGINS

Augustus Smith was still most amenable to the project. Trinity House minutes record that, on 1 August he wrote that 'he shall be happy to afford every facility for quarrying granite on the Island of St Mary's required in the erection of the proposed Stone Light House on the Bishops [sic] Rock; adding that altho he shall want no charge for the stone itself, it will be necessary that certain stipulations should be entered into as to the mode and manner in which the operations are to be conducted, and which had better be arranged between our Clerk of the Works, and his Steward Mr James, with whom the former should also communicate in respect of the locality best suited to procure the necessary material'.[10] In response, Trinity House were pleased to acknowledge Smith's offer, and accepted.

By 5 September, Nicholas Douglass had done three tides of work on Bishop Rock and, that day, had managed about an hour's work in the lowest part of the foundation. By 10 September they had had two good tides of work in the lowest part of the foundation, and a template had been made for the first stone which was to be prepared on St Mary's.

He and Mr James had chosen a convenient place on Peninnis to the north of Pulpit Rock to quarry the stone for the intended lighthouse. He had also found a piece of ground for the purpose of working the stone on Rat Island. From here the stone would be taken out to Bishop Rock. Unfortunately, as seen below, Douglass seemed to have forgotten that permission from Augustus Smith would be needed, and this oversight did not go down too well.

On Rat Island there is a circular structure which local tradition claims originates from the building work. It seems to be very likely this was the template for the first granite tower as the measurements of the diameter (approximately 30 feet, three inches minimum external diameter) fit, more or less, those given by James Walker. According to local tradition, it was also used in the building of the 1880s improvements to the tower.

Plans of the workshop on St Mary's show a granite building which is still there today. The ground floor was used as a store while a carpenter's shop and office were located on the first floor. To the north of the building was the smith's shop, with the mason's shed to the right of that. There was also a lime kiln, now long gone, and a harbour office.

Nicholas Douglass wrote from St Agnes on 23 September 1850 saying that he intended to remove the workmen from Rosevear in the ensuing week as he did not foresee much more work being done at Bishop Rock that season.

One month later, on 23 October, Augustus Smith wrote to Trinity House suggesting that the granite required for the lighthouse might be more advantageously obtained on the mainland of Cornwall than on Scilly. Quarrying operations were suspended while they considered the matter, concluding that it would be best to obtain the stone from Lamorna and Carnsew quarries in Cornwall.

Writing in 1907, J. G. Uren claimed that Nicholas Douglass (who he erroneously refers to as William) was at 'logger-heads' with Augustus Smith over the quarrying of stone for the lighthouse, and 'shook his fist', while Smith claimed the stone was his and it was not to be quarried until certain terms had been met. But this conflicts with contemporary accounts which show, as seen above, that Smith had been helpful to Trinity House. It was on other matters that relations between the two parties became rather strained, as will be seen.

In late December 1850, bearing in mind the saga with the iron lighthouse, Trinity House asked Walker whether he wanted Nicholas Douglass to be employed as Superintendent of the Works at Bishop Rock again. In his reply of 3 January 1851 he said he knew of no one better qualified. They were satisfied with this and, by April, Douglass had found accommodation at Bank, St Mary's with his wife Alice, son James, who acted as Assistant Engineer (he was known as Cap'n Jim by the workmen)

and niece Jane Jolly. Nicholas's Resident Engineer, John McConnochie found lodgings in Church Street with Edward and Sarah Banfield and their two young daughters, Anna and Mary.

By now, Nicholas Douglass was aged 51, so much of the 'hands on' work fell to James.

In early February 1851 Walker obtained a tender from W. & J. Freeman, who owned the Lamorna and Carnsew quarries, to supply 100 tons of granite for Bishop Rock lighthouse at 1s 6d per foot cube. This would be delivered to St Mary's quay, and the unloading undertaken by Trinity House Corporation, which they accepted.

Trouble had started to brew between Augustus Smith and Trinity House. Douglass's failure to obtain permission for the area on Rat Island to work stone had been discovered. Smith wrote to Trinity House on 14 February from St James Place, London, complaining that Nicholas Douglass 'has proceeded to excavate some ground adjoining the Sheds already erected for Other Buildings of a similar kind, without having made any previous communication to him on the subject.'[11] He would not agree to this work until Douglass communicated with him. So Walker was instructed to look into the matter and to act upon it and, in the meantime, Trinity House were compelled to send their regrets to Smith.

STRUCTURAL WORK BEGINS

Bad weather delayed the start of work on the lighthouse but, by 15 April 1851, Burges and McConnochie were able to report that the men had started work cutting the upper portions of Bishop Rock, and fixing a trammel (a gauge for setting up a machine correctly) on its centre.

Although it was a physical impossibility, due to a lack of suitable surface rock, it has been claimed that a coffer dam was built around the rock to keep out the sea, thus letting the workmen toil away unimpeded.[12] But this was not the case. Confusion has arisen with the coffer dam built at the Eddystone lighthouse, a point verified by the late Captain Michael Tarrant of Trinity House Corporation.[13]

Some of the men coming to Scilly to work on the lighthouse often lodged on St Mary's. The 1851 census lists Cornish stonemasons, stonecutters, and miners living in Hugh Town, many of whom probably worked on Bishop Rock or on Rat Island. Others lived in the barracks on Rosevear (not included in the census).

Elder Brethren, Captains Farrer, Owen and Drew, a Capt Shuttleworth and members of the Light Committee, undertook an inspection of Scilly (and other places) in July 1851. They took pilot Francis Pender, who lived at Buzza, on board their boat for Bishop Rock. They:

> Anchored abreast of the landing place at Rosevear. Landed and viewed the Barracks of the Workmen; and the Workshops. 3.00pm Landed on the Bishop: found 18 men at work cutting the Rock to receive the foundation stones.

They were most concerned to learn that they and Nicholas Douglass worked on Sundays.

> 4.30pm Anchored off the Pier at St Mary's, landed and looked at the Workshops and Shed at the Pier Head where the stone will be prepared for the Bishop Light House. The Shed and Workshops are 700 feet distant from the nearest dwelling. Some arrangement is necessary to procure Medical attendance for our People here.[14]

*Quarry at Lamorna from an old postcard.*

Trinity House remained rather aggrieved that Douglass and the men worked on Sundays. Walker was ordered to ensure it did not happen as a general rule, unless urgently required. But the weather had been so rough that no work could be undertaken during early August and, no doubt, was why the work continued on Sundays. This practice also took place when constructing the Eddystone lighthouse.

On Friday 29 August the Corporation Committee landed on St Mary's and met with Walker to inspect progress at Bishop Rock for themselves. They arrived at 1.50pm at low water and so had a good view of progress on the lowest part of the Rock.

### LOSS OF VESSEL WITH GRANITE

Bad weather was not the only cause of delay. A major and tragic setback occurred at sea. On 5 September W. & J. Freeman wrote regarding the delay in delivery of 100 tons of their granite for the lighthouse. This was caused by the loss of the vessel and cargo in June, presumably somewhere between Lamorna and Scilly, when all crew perished.* Other stones had been prepared in lieu of those lost and were in the course of shipment. However, should a further supply of stone be needed, they would have to alter the terms to 1s 9d per cubic foot on shipboard at Scilly, instead of 1s 6d 'on account of the scrapping (scrappling/scraping?) of stones to such fixed dimensions, and the strict attention required to the quality (several stones having been rejected) being attended with more expense than they had anticipated, - independently of the Risk of Shipping'.[15]

### DANGEROUS WORKING CONDITIONS

On 29 September Burges wrote saying two landings had been made on Bishop Rock the previous week, but that the men had not been able to work at the bottom course. This initial work was especially dangerous as there was no shelter from sudden sea swells and wave action (and no coffer dam).

The atrocious conditions in which the men had to work was awesome, and their nerves must have been sorely tested. There was no opportunity to escape from the situation for a short respite; they had to remain at their posts until the working day was over.

The men would often be compelled to cling to one another 'with a grip so intense as sometimes to cause flesh wounds'.[16] Even getting on and off the rock was far from easy and it could be late before the men reached their barracks on Rosevear due to unsuitable boarding conditions. One can only imagine how they felt.

---

* Unfortunately, no further information on this event has been found.

The lowest (foundation) stone, on the north west side, and one foot below low-water spring-tide, was intended to be laid in 1851, but this was not carried out until 1852, as seen below, due to unfavourable sea conditions. Fortunately, due to an uneven rock base, this did not prevent work at higher levels. Throughout the building work, a method of dowelling (invented by Nicholas Douglass) rather than dove-tailing the granite was used.[17]

Towards the end of December 1851 Walker said that Nicholas Douglass and his son would return to Scilly in the ensuing months to resume operations at any time, depending on the state of the weather. During some of the time James Douglass was not employed on Bishop Rock, he was engaged in erecting a beacon on the Woolpack rock, an outcrop south of the Garrison on St Mary's.

Nicholas and James Douglass returned to Scilly in March 1852, the same month as the lighting apparatus was delivered to Blackwall. On 14 July, the first stone of the fifth course was laid, while on Friday 30 July, the foundation or lowest stone of all was laid. These were momentous enough occasions for them to be recorded in a special plaque later put up in the lighthouse, together with other key dates.

*James Douglass*
INSTITUTION OF
CIVIL ENGINEERS

Due to the dangerous nature of laying this foundation stone, no man would go into the prepared hole unless Douglass went too; 'a party of masons - led, of course, by a Douglass - had to set the lowest stones of the work; when someone placed above them on watch would shout out that there was a big sea coming; and, suddenly, would burst upon them a tremendous wave by which they were immersed to a depth of a dozen feet, they clinging, meanwhile, to iron stanchions fixed in the rock, and emerging at last breathless, and sometimes utterly exhausted, with the prospect of a similar experience shortly afterwards'.[18] Occasionally, a man would be washed off the rock into the swirling sea and had to be rescued – James Douglass was usually credited with this bravery. He was always

the last to leave the rock, seeing his men safely into the boat, and then would cast off the ropes and swim out to join them.

The laying of the foundation stone was clearly not straightforward which is why it took place a long time after work had begun. But Trinity House officials apparently lost patience and exclaimed, 'I do not suppose you ever expect to live to get that stone in'. Somewhat rattled, James Douglass retorted, 'I do, and remember that I have a father still alive'.[19]

The quality of life for the men on Rosevear, who were mostly Cornish, was variable. The island has nothing between it and the power of the Atlantic Ocean, with the exception of the Crebinicks and the Retarrier Ledges. The rough weather and storms that could suddenly blow in meant that they became cut off from all means of communication. The sea would be whipped up into a seething mass of foaming water which would come crashing down upon the small exposed island and its barracks sheltering the men from the very worst it could produce. Also, as James Douglass commented years later, on what he might have felt was a more positive note, the workmen ' had excellent opportunities of watching what was going on at the "Bishop" during storms, from the top of a cairn (carn) about 40 feet above high water'.[20] Some comfort. According to the Ordnance Survey, the actual height of the carn is 47 feet.

Bad weather prevented deliveries too, and food could become in such short supply that the men resorted to eating raw limpets. In clement weather, they were able to grow vegetables which accompanied the fish they caught. They also had an abundance of wild birds, most of which were puffins and their eggs.[21] Had he discovered this practice, Augustus Smith would have been greatly displeased as it was at odds with his instructions not to disturb the island's wildlife!

There is also the often-told tale of a grand ball on Rosevear to which islanders were invited. 'The sheds were all cleared of their contents, brilliantly illuminated, and decorated with bunting, and, at the expected hour, the visitors arrived in innumerable boats. Dancing was kept up until early morning (when the guests rowed back by moonlight) to the accompaniment of the barrack band, led by James Douglass, who played well on the flute'.[22] On another musical note, a blacksmith, who had been compelled to stay alone on Rosevear one day, thought he heard some evocative music and assumed it was his fellow workmates returning. But it was not, and he described the music as 'not of this world'.[23]

As indicated above, not all the workmen lived on Rosevear. On 9 July 1852, mason James Hawkin rented from the Ordnance Board, Room No. 7 in the Infantry Barracks on the Garrison for £2 per year, while Henry Angwin rented Rooms 5 and 6 from 10 September, also for £2 per year (he had been lodging with George and Mary Sherris at Bank). Those employed in the workshops on Rat Island would have lived on St Mary's.

RELATIONS WITH AUGUSTUS SMITH DETERIORATE

It would seem that more space was needed at the workshops. The deliveries of granite from the mainland took up a large area. But, by now, relations with Augustus Smith had deteriorated. On 9 September 1852 he wrote to Trinity House saying he was sorry he could not provide more space needed for the mason's working yard on St Mary's for work in progress, 'the portion already occupied is very much to his inconvenience'. He further said he was 'induced to concede the use of these Premises as a Mason's Yard on the understanding that the Granite was to be procured on the Islands from a Quarry to be fairly opened for that purpose, that as it is he has no such benefit while he suffers much inconvenience and requesting therefore that the Works be confined in future to the present enclosure, and that orders may be conveyed to Mr Douglas [sic] to that effect, instead of the outside space being encumbered as at present by large accumulation of Granite blocks'.[24]

Trinity House referred back to the letter of Smith's of 23 October 1850 in which he suggested the granite required might be more advantageously obtained on the mainland of Cornwall – it would seem that Smith had forgotten this and needed a gentle reminder.

At the end of 1852, on 24 December, James Douglass left Scilly for Stella near Newcastle-on-Tyne. He had obtained employment as manager of R. J. & R. Laycock's railway works.[25]

On the departure of James Douglass, Nicholas had applied to have his second son, William, replace him. He was 22 years old and had been trained in the millwrighting and engineering trades, and had spent 12 months assisting at Scilly without pay. Initially, Nicholas requested £2 per week pay for William, which was 20s less than James, but he subsequently felt £3 per week was a fairer salary. But the Corporation refused this and went with his first suggestion. It was not until April 1854, that William's salary was raised from £2 per week to £150 per year.

By mid-January 1853, it would seem that Trinity House had managed to appease Augustus Smith as both parties approved a draft agreement for the future occupation of the workshops at St Mary's, with a fixed rent of £20 p.a. The term was to be for the continuance of the works, with power given to the Corporation to use as much of the stone chippings as they might require, and for setting up a Watch Box on the premises.

TUG, BARGES AND OTHER MATTERS

James Walker felt that, for the success of the work over the next few years, it would be desirable to have a steam tug of from 25 to 30 horse power, and also three stone barges to carry stone from St Mary's to Bishop Rock, plus an old lighter to be moored in St Mary's harbour as a coal hulk for the tug. The barges might be built at St Mary's, and Nicholas

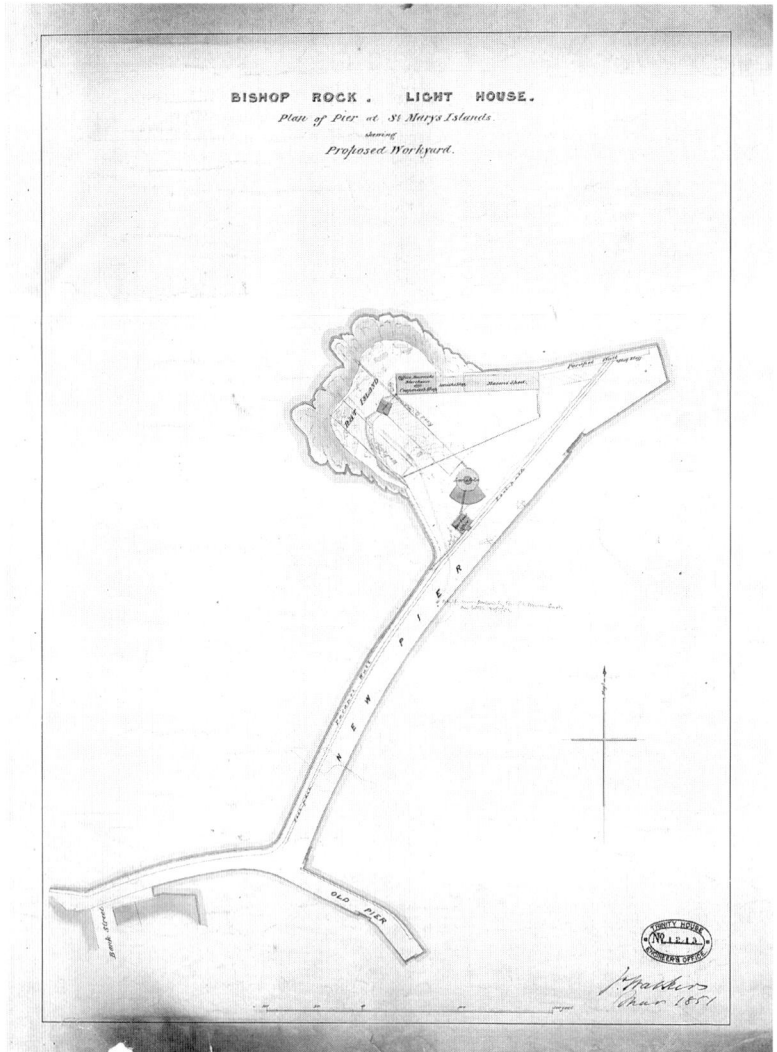

Douglass had prepared a drawing and specifications which were to be shown to an experienced shipbuilder. Tenders could then be obtained from St Mary's and elsewhere, while a steam tug would probably be purchased at Newcastle or London, so long as it was strong and fit for the works. The tug and barges were to be at St Mary's by 1 May.

In January 1853, Walker received a letter from T. & W. Smith of Newcastle saying they could acquire a steam tug of 25hp built on the Tyne with the engine and boilers made locally. Under a year old, it would cost £850. Otherwise, they could get a boat built to order for £1,100 which would be of superior quality, but not ready in less than four months. The other was available immediately.

Trinity House decided on the new vessel and asked Walker to

negotiate with T. & W. Smith to build one not exceeding the £1,100, and to be ready in May. If it was not to be ready in time, they must provide a suitable vessel for work on Bishop Rock until it was.

In due course, T. & W. Smith came forward with plans to build a tug of 56 tons, 25 horse steam power, and sheathed with Muntz Patent Metal, for £1,500, and which would be delivered in May or they would provide another vessel until ready. Although this exceeded the original plan by £400, it was accepted by Trinity House and, appropriately, it was to be named *Bishop*.

The subject of Sunday work reared its head again, and Trinity House told Walker 'that the Masonry at the Rock being now 3 Feet above Low Water, - it is considered that there is no longer any necessity that work should, on any occasion be performed on a Sunday'.[26] However, within a few days, Walker responded to this by saying that the three feet in question applied only to spring tides, and that the masonry was still generally one to two feet under the level of low water. He asked whether they could work on Sundays until it was three feet above low tide? They agreed to this but stipulated that work on Sundays must stop once the level had been reached.

After minor alterations to Douglass's specifications for stone barges, he suggested three names of first class builders on St Mary's – William Mumford, and brothers John and Thomas Edwards. At Penzance there was only one shipyard, that of M. Mathews & Co, mostly undertaking repairs. Tenders were invited, with the stipulation that one barge must be ready by 1 May, the others by 1 June.

Thomas Edwards won the contract to build them and it was signed on 1 March, although payment of £1,050 was not forthcoming until December. His shipyard was on Town Beach to the east of that owned by William Mumford. Edward's sawpits and timber stacks etc were on the site where the Methodist Church now stands. His brother John's shipyard was on the eastern end of Porthcressa beach.

Towards the end of March, a coal hulk was authorised to be taken to Scilly in readiness for the steam tug *Bishop*.

It was during 1853 that Nicholas Douglass made observations of the movements of the waves at Bishop Rock to see how they might affect the lighthouse. They were found to have the following heights:

8 feet from hollow to crest, number 35 in one mile, and 8 per minute
15 feet from hollow to crest, number 5 & 6 in one mile, and 5 per minute
20 feet from hollow to crest, number 3 in one mile, and 4 per minute

The first two observations were made from the rock 'and were estimated by means of a reef, three-quarters of a mile distant. The last, or those upon the 20-feet waves, which are the highest he has observed there,

Sketch of Back Guard Room, and Prison, St Mary's, Scilly Islands.

were made from a vessel.'[27] Happily, it was concluded that these waves, however frequent, would not be detrimental to the lighthouse.

In early February 1854, all occupants of the Infantry Barracks on the Garrison, including Henry Angwin and James Hawkin were given notice to quit as the premises was required by the Collector of Customs (responsible for the Coastguard service) for additional staff. They were permitted to stay until 24 March which was an improvement on the initial plan that had been for instant evacuation. Towards the end of the month, James Hawkin asked to rent 'the small detached unoccupied Building known as the "Back Guard Room & Prison". This House being at present a mere shell, Walls and Roof; the mason proposes at his own expense to put in Window-frame, Sash & Glass, to mend the plaster and floors, and to leave the Repairs standing, when he shall be required to give

it up.'[28] Hawkins received permission for this at a rent of 10s p.a.

The site of this building can be found at Steval Point up against the Garrison wall at SV 89525 10360. By 1888 it was ruinous, although its north wall survives for a length of 5.2 metres and a width of 0.76 metres. It is faced with uncoursed rubble. The seaward west wall, which was part of the Garrison fortifications, has an internal height of 1.43m. A vertical strip of mortar, 6.9m southwards from the corner indicates the south end of the building.

On 26 June the cutter *Belinda*, full of limestone and en route from Cardiff to Cork, hit Bishop Rock in thick fog. Fortunately, all crew were rescued. It is possible that the workmen were on Rosevear and were able to see something of the aftermath.

James Douglass returned to Scilly in June 1854 and married Mary Tregarthen on 6 July. She was the second daughter of James Tregarthen, a shipowner whose brother, Hugh Tregarthen was the Trinity House Agent. He returned to Stella with his bride in 1855, after the birth of their first child, James Nicholas.

At the end of the working season in October, the steam tug *Bishop* went to Blackwall for repairs and service in the London district until it was required on Scilly for the next season. In November, Seaward & Capel tendered £91 16s 3d for the repairs needed, which was accepted.

To 31 December 1854, £24,500 had been spent so far on building Bishop Rock lighthouse.

By January 1855 Trinity House had decided to make some alterations to the lighthouse. The light was to burn at 110 feet, the height of the tower was to be increased by 10 feet and the diameter of the lantern was to be 14 feet. Walker sent them an estimate of this additional cost, £4,000, with the comment that it would make the lighthouse walls stronger. This met with approval.

At about this time Trinity House also noted 'the zeal, perseverance and skill' of Nicholas Douglass during the three seasons in which the lighthouse had been in the course of erection. Fifty guineas were presented to him, and ten guineas to his son William for the assistance he had given his father. It would seem that James received nothing, despite being actively involved in the initial stages.

In the absence of James Walker, on 9 April, Mr James Cooper wrote to say that Douglass had landed on Bishop Rock on 31 March to fix the derrick mast. After the winter months, all the stones were found to be perfectly secure, which must have been a huge relief, but he had not been able to land since.

TRINITY HOUSE INSPECTIONS

On Friday 22 June the Light Committee took William Douglass on board their vessel from St Mary's pier. They and two barges of stone went to Bishop Rock but the swell was too big to land. However they were able to observe the works and recorded in their minutes: 'The building shews well out of the water, and appears very solid and substantial. The wooden derrick had then been carried away a second time, it is presumed by the rebound of the breakers off the Tower. Douglass is of opinion that recourse may be had to a wrought iron derrick'.[29] The following day, the Committee tried to land again on Bishop Rock but the swell was still too great, so they gave up and went to the Lizard lighthouse.

The 'South Coast Committee' did manage to land on the rock on 11 September, and observed them completing the 19th course.[30]

Robert Maybee, the nineteenth century Scillonian poet, worked on Bishop Rock lighthouse from 1855:

> In 1855 I engaged to work on the Trinity House Works, to build a lighthouse on Bishop Rock. It was a very pleasant summer and I was pleased with my employment. The labourers and bargemen were paid off on the last day of November, but the stonecutters, carpenters and blacksmiths were all kept on three weeks later'.[31]

During the winter months he worked for a farmer on St Agnes and then left to continue work on the lighthouse. He described the nature of his work as 'taking stones from St Mary's to build the Lighthouse on the Bishop Rock'.[32]

The Light Committee made another inspection on Scilly in May 1856, taking with them from the mainland 45 tons of coal to St Agnes. They visited both Bishop Rock and the workshop and stores on St Mary's, and everything seemed satisfactory. But Nicholas Douglass complained that the contractors were not keeping him supplied with stone. This matter became a bone of contention and, in November, Walker told Trinity House that if stones for the courses of the lighthouse had been sent more regularly by the contractors, another floor or storey of the tower might have been built by them that autumn. But they refused to accept this and told him that it was he who was responsible as he had failed to tell them of the contractors' 'dilatoriness'.

The Committee made another visit on Friday 26 September. There was too much swell to land on Bishop Rock, but they saw the 34th course completed and the 44th course already on shore. Stone for the 47th course had not been received but the yard was blocked up with that for the 64th and higher courses.

They also met with Augustus Smith, who complained that three unspecified conditions had not been attended to. Also, 'Mr Smith appears to be afraid that Mr Douglass will remove the buildings at St Mary's (when done with) as he has removed those at Rose Vear'.[33] So from this, we learn that Rosevear was no longer required for operations by now (1856). Substantial ruins of the buildings survived for decades and, even now, they are features in the landscape. But Douglass must have stripped them of all fittings and fixtures, probably including the roof slates, and dismantled any wooden structures, for Smith to have made this observation.

Mr Poulter wrote on 16 October reminding the Corporation that the lighting apparatus for Bishop Rock had been at the Wharf at Blackwall since March 1852.

Trinity House decided in January 1857 the time had come to invite tenders for another lantern. These were considered in early March:

|  | ⁶/₈" glass | ⁵/₈" glass |
|---|---|---|
| Messrs Simpson | £1,594 | £1,563 |
| Messrs Lawrence | £1,588 | £1,555 |
| Mr Wilkins | £1,371 16s | £1,317 1s 10d |
| Mr DeVille | £2,223 10s | £2,168 10s |

The tender of Wilkins & Co was accepted and, in April, a contract was entered into with them for 11 weeks, for constructing the lantern at a cost of £1,371 16s. They were also to make a lantern for Whitby lighthouse.

Wilkins had written to Trinity House on 7 March saying that the Bishop Rock lighthouse apparatus at Blackwall, procured in 1850, was ready to fit up there for experimentation in the presence of their scientific advisor, Prof. Michael Faraday. So the Deputy Master and other Brethren went to Blackwall to see the effect of the apparatus in April. They continued experimenting with different types of light over the next couple of months, and concluded that the brightest light available was needed.

On 23 March 1857 the future lighthouse engineer, William Tregarthen Douglass, son of James and Mary, and grandson of Nicholas, was born.

The Light Committee went to St Mary's on Monday 22 June to make another inspection of the works, finding all the courses of stone, except two upper ones, prepared and ready. Doors, window frames and ladders were in a forward state; the wood lining for the inside of the tower was of very fine wainscoting, panelled and of good workmanship. Again, they could not land on Bishop Rock but saw the 54th course completed.

In early July 1857, Douglass proposed that a few men should stay on the lighthouse as soon as the bedroom courses were set. At first, Trinity House was not prepared to incur the responsibility for these men, and he was told to make a further report when the sleeping room was complete. Later that month, Walker discussed Douglass's reasons for the workmen remaining on Bishop Rock; ' there is much less probability of an accident from some of the Workpeople remaining at the Bishop Rock Light House, than in building it and in the passage to and from it and landing'.[34] Happier with this explanation, Trinity House was now able to give their agreement, and so we see the first habitation of the lighthouse.

On 28 August 1857 the last stone was laid at Bishop Rock lighthouse, thus completing this stage of construction. It must have been a momentous occasion for all concerned, the unrelenting seas having made this aspect of work the worst part for many men.

Now that the end was in sight, Trinity House had to make some provision for the accommodation of future lighthouse keepers. Bearing in mind his previous offer of housing, they decided to write to Augustus Smith in October asking for land to be made available on an island for that purpose. His response was not forthcoming until prompted the following January, as seen below.

The strength and durability of the lighthouse was soon to be tested. During a bad gale on 7 October 1857, William Douglass happened to be on Bishop Rock. Reporting this matter to Trinity House later that month, Walker informed them that Douglass could scarcely feel a tremor in the tower, and that not more than a gallon of spray water had come over the pedestal of the lantern. Local pilots claimed there had not been such a storm for 40 years, so the stability of the tower was felt to have been truly tested. Such optimism was not to last.

THE LIGHTING APPARATUS

Further experiments to test the lighting apparatus for Bishop Rock took place during October at Hornchurch, Essex. A number of errors were noted by Faraday and, after the lamp burner had consequently been lowered ³/₄ inch, further tests were carried out on the evening of Tuesday 10 November, at 6.30pm. The test between 7.02pm and 7.33pm was to evaluate the effectiveness of a fixed light and that between 7.33pm and 8.09pm a revolving light.

At 6.30pm the light was shown on the tower of the church and fixed for half an hour, after which, the following took place, as recorded by Faraday and Trinity House:[35]

2 minutes darkness during which 2 rockets will be thrown up.
- 7.02pm the great lens with zones fixed, for 5 minutes, 2 minutes darkness, during which 2 rockets will be thrown up
- 7.09pm the seven reflectors fixed, for 5 minutes, 2 minutes darkness, during which 2 rockets will be thrown up
- 7.16pm the great lens fixed, for 5 minutes, 2 minutes darkness, during which 2 rockets will be thrown up
- 7.23pm the 7 reflectors fixed for 5 minutes, 5 minutes darkness, during which 2 rockets will be thrown up

The apparatus will commence revolving at 7.33 being arranged as follows,

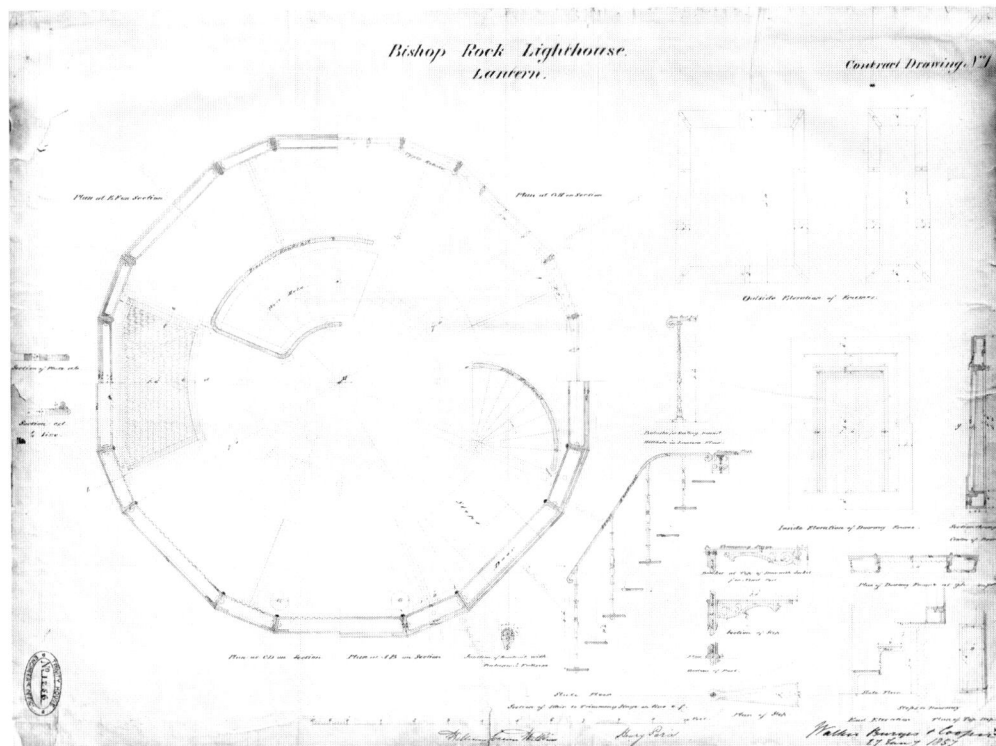

*Bishop Rock Lighthouse.*
*Lantern.*

*Contract Drawing. N.9*

viz 1st – 7 Reflectors and their Lamps on one face, occupying one
fourth of the circle.

2nd –Two Buchanness arrangements (each of three Reflectors ⊞ )
the two occupying one fourth of the circle.

3rd – The Great Lens $37^1/_2$ x 29 inches, occupying one fourth of
the circle.

4th – Four Bishop Lenses etc occupying one fourth of the circle.

- at 7.33. The first series of Revolutions consisting of 3
Revolutions of 40 seconds each. 5 minutes darkness, during
which 2 rockets will be thrown up.

- at: 7.40 2nd Series of Revolutions, consisting of 2 revolutions
of 4 minutes each, 5 minutes darkness, during which 2 rockets
will be thrown up.

- 7.53 3rd Series of Revolutions, consisting of 2 Revolutions of
8 minutes each.

- 8.09pm experiments concluded.

Faraday was, on the whole, pleased with the experiments. The
lowering of the burner level, in his opinion, had added to the value of the
Bishop's lenses, and superseded the Buchanness reflectors in power,
although 'did not endure so long in the eye'. [36]

*Plan of the
Lantern Room
1857.*
TRINITY HOUSE

In November, the Court decided that the light should be fixed rather than revolving, and exhibited by means of a catadioptrical (where rays from the light source form a beam by means of both reflection and refraction) apparatus of the first order. But the following month, some of the Elder Brethren dissented from this for the following reasons:[37]

1. That whereas the Bishop light being a fixed one and within 4½ nautical miles of the light on St Agnes renders the continuance of the latter, no longer necessary for navigating the channel and it may therefore be discontinued (as the entire distance on a line between the Lizard and the Bishop Light is illuminated independently of St Agnes) under which circumstances there will be five consecutive lights on the fixed principle exhibited within a space of 100 miles.

2. That whereas from the earliest period the western light on the Scilly Islands has been of a revolving character, and doubtless so arranged to unmistakably distinguish it from the fixed light on Ushant. The said western light under the Court's resolution will now be very similar to Ushant, and may consequently lead vessels entering the British Channel into danger, and more particularly so when with either of those Light Houses bearing East and distant 16 or 17 miles, the soundings are nearly the same both in depth and character of the bottom.

(Signed) William Piggott
Charles Farquharson

Elder Brethren James Drew and John Fenwick then stated grounds on which they supported the above points. Trinity House had taken the decision to have a revolving light back in 1850, and the apparatus was obtained and delivered to Blackwall. Also, the relative merits of a fixed and of a revolving light were at least three to one in favour of the revolving. A lighthouse was to be erected on Godrevy bearing from the Bishop East distant 48 miles. The light should be different from Godrevy so as not to be mistaken in bad weather. Godrevy, they argued, could be mistaken for Bishop Rock lighthouse.

But the Court remained firm, and it was decided that the fixed catadioptric light on Bishop Rock was to be exhibited on 1 September 1858. Firms were to be invited to tender for a contract to construct the apparatus. What happened to the 1850 model at Blackwall is not recorded.

LIGHTHOUSE KEEPERS' DWELLINGS

Not having heard from Augustus Smith, Trinity House wrote again, in January 1858, regarding land for the keepers' dwellings. His reply on 9th was rather curt, saying that they did not need any extra land from him. He also took the opportunity of further requesting that his premises, which they had occupied on Rat Island for purposes connected with the erection of the lighthouse, might be speedily restored to him.

Despite these difficulties, Douglass was able to report a few days later that 'a most eligible spot for the erection of the dwellings for the keepers of the Bishop Rock Light House may be obtained upon Land at St Mary's belonging to the Ordnance Office now in the occupation of Mr Murdoch, the Master Gunner, it was referred to Mr Walker to make enquiry of the Ordnance Department if any of the land adverted to can be obtained for the purposes of the Bishop Light House Dwellings'.[38]

This enquiry was successful and, in mid-February, Douglass was able to inform them that land for four houses on the east side of Hugh Hill had been found five minutes walk from the brow of the hill from which the lighthouse could be seen without being exposed to the full power of the prevailing storms. As the land was owned by the Duchy of Cornwall, permission then had to be sought from them.

On 11 March Walker informed Trinity House that he had conferred with Mr Gardiner, the Duchy of Cornwall secretary, as to the terms for the $1^{1}/_{2}$ acres of ground at Hugh Hill, for the dwellings, and that he proposed a rent of £10 p.a. for a term of 99 years. The ground was to be surrendered in case of being required for purposes of public defence and the Duchy would pay a fair value for the dwellings and work that may have been done by the Corporation at the time of surrender, should it happen.

However, Mr Farrer, from the Office of the Board of Trade, felt the rent seemed very high and could a smaller sum be agreed? To this, Walker responded 'that the Land in question having a Building Frontage of 400 Feet the Rent asked by the Duchy of Cornwall is moderate'.[39] With this agreed, Walker was informed that the dimensions for the four houses were to be the same as those of the Portland keepers in Dorset. They were to be in two pairs instead of four separate dwellings as it was more convenient for the apportionment of the ground. Expenditure on the houses was not to exceed £500, and Nicholas Douglass was to be contracted to build them. The lease for the land arrived in June.

In the meantime, tenders for making the lighting apparatus had arrived, and Wilkins & Co's one for £1,313 10s, to include fittings and cost of transport, was accepted. Although it was not the lowest price, it was thought the product would be superior. He was also to make apparatus for the Needles lighthouse. At the end of March, he had put forward Dominick Pope and John Brittain as his sureties 'for the due performance of their contract in providing and fitting the Dioptic Apparatus' for Bishop Rock and the Needles. They were accepted and a contract and bond was prepared. Messrs Lepaute of Paris were asked to make the optical parts. As with the iron lighthouse, a Fresnel lens was chosen.

An easy landing was made at the lighthouse on Saturday 12 June 1858 by the Light Committee. They noted that the glass in the lantern had a green appearance. The stairs were ready to be put in place, as was the woodwork for the other rooms. Completion of the lighthouse was estimated to be three months away. With the end of the work in sight, it was suggested that the workmen could be transferred to Hanois lighthouse to work there.

Whilst working on Bishop Rock, two men applied to be lighthouse keepers, and they were recommended by Nicholas Douglass. They were Henry Williams, age 35, single, and who had worked with Douglass for nine years, and John Williams, who had a wife and six children. Both men had worked on the lighthouse from its commencement. The Committee decided to recommend them for the posts. Edward Penn, aged 58, also applied for the job. He was 'now Master of the Bishop'[40] and had worked for Douglass for more than 20 years. But a post for him was not to be forthcoming. He was probably considered too old by Trinity House as they tended to prefer young men for their lighthouse keepers.

MINOR IRRITATIONS

Minor irritations started to arise. A Trinity House Committee had been to Scilly recently, and Walker was informed that they considered the position in which the keepers' dwellings were to be built was objectionable. They were now to be built as nearly as possible parallel with the Ordnance Road, and a little nearer the entrance gate than had been planned.

In early July Faraday wrote saying that the apparatus supplied by Wilkins & Co for Bishop Rock was 'very unfavourable as regards the Colour and quality of the Glass employed in the manufacture of the said Apparatus'.[41] A copy of this letter was sent to Wilkins & Co with the instruction that the defective portion must be replaced, and that Faraday would give advice on what the portions removed were to be replaced with. Faraday made further investigations, discussing the matter with an expert in Paris. Fortunately, it would seem that the Frenchman allayed his fears, and he was consequently prepared to accept the Wilkins apparatus. It arrived at St Mary's in mid-July, and Nicholas Douglass said that he hoped the lighthouse would be finished within one month.

Augustus Smith was still expressing concern at Trinity House's occupation of his premises on St Mary's. At the end of July, he wrote complaining he had never had a reply from them in response to his letter on the subject, and that he now wanted the premises on the pier for his own purposes. They decided to write to him expressing regrets. They explained that the delay in vacating was due to the prolonged period of erection of the lighthouse, and therefore a final settlement had not been possible. But Smith, not prepared to be lenient in this matter, responded by asking for compensation settlement due to him on account of the Corporation's occupancy of the workyard.

### THE FIRST LIGHTHOUSE KEEPERS

The Light Committee appointed the following men in August as the very first Bishop Rock lighthouse keepers:

J. N. Watson – Principal Keeper
Thomas Hallam – Assistant Keeper
John Williams – Assistant Keeper
Henry Williams – Assistant Keeper

They would spend a month on the lighthouse before being allowed shore leave. Three keepers would be there at any one time.
Keepers were divided into different categories:

- PRINCIPAL KEEPER (PK) – promoted from Assistant Keeper when vacancies arose.
- ASSISTANT KEEPER (AK) – appointed to a lighthouse on completion of Supernumerary Assistant Keeper training.
- SUPERNUMERARY ASSISTANT KEEPER (SAK/SK) – a new recruit to the service who spent about 12 months on probation moving from lighthouse to lighthouse taking over duties for other keepers who were sick or on leave. A keeper's first job.
- OCCASIONAL KEEPER (OK) – locally employed relief keepers for when short-staffed.

A free uniform was supplied annually plus rent-free accommodation or a housing allowance, a rock allowance for those keepers assigned to rock lighthouses such as Bishop Rock, and a daily victualling allowance for the period on the lighthouse. Food rations for the whole month had to be taken onto the lighthouse by each keeper, and 'iron rations' were for emergency use only. This use only became necessary if a relief could not be undertaken due to bad weather – this could last for weeks sometimes.

### THE LIGHT IS OPERATIONAL

At last, a decade or so after construction of the ill-fated iron structure had begun, mariners were to benefit from a light on the Western Rocks. Hugh Tregarthen informed the Light Committee on 16 August that he had made arrangements for the first exhibition of the Bishop Rock light to be made on the evening of 1 September 1858. Although contemporary records do not give an account of this occasion, it must have been a very special moment when the light was shown for the very first time. After the event, on 2 September, Tregarthen wrote to the Light Committee saying that it 'shewed a very brilliant Light'.[42]

Prince Albert, when addressing Trinity House about the lighthouse, said it was 'a triumph of engineering skill and perseverance'.[43]

At a Court held at Trinity House on 7 September, great pleasure was expressed at the completion of Bishop Rock lighthouse, and a resolution was passed:

> The important undertaking of constructing a Light House upon the Bishop Rock having been brought to a conclusion by the exhibition of Light therefrom on the night of 1st Instant, the Court avail themselves of the earliest opportunity to record the high sense they entertain of the good services rendered by every person engaged in this difficult operation.
>
> The Court desire to express their warmest approbation of the scientific plans and arrangements of Mr James Walker and his able assistants Messrs Burges and Cooper, and of the great assiduity with which they have superintended the progress of the work.
>
> The Court desire especially to reward the exertions of Mr Nicholas Douglass, the Corporation's Superintending Engineer of the Works, to whose intrepid courage and energy, combined with the coolest judgement and forethought, may be ascribed the successful termination of a work carried on during a period of eight years under circumstances at all times dangerous, and frequently of great peril, without loss of life, or the occurrence of any accident of a serious nature.
>
> The Court anxious to testify their sense of the merits of Mr Douglass in their bringing to a conclusion an enterprise which in less energetic hands might have been much protracted, at great additional expense, unanimously resolve, that a grant of £300 equal to his salary for one year, be made to Mr Nicholas Douglas [sic] in acknowledgement of the skill, zeal, and undaunted perseverance he has manifested in the construction of the Bishop Rock Light House, and that the same be submitted to the Board of Trade for their Lordships' sanctions.[44]

Two days later, at another Court sitting, Capt Sullivan commented, 'This should I think be approved, as it has been a work of great danger and difficulty, and from all I have heard of Mr Douglass, he must be a very superior man for works of this kind – the pay for such work has not been high for an Assistant Engineer.'[45]

The construction of the lighthouse in such a difficult position, and in

*The completed lighthouse in 1858.* ILLUSTRATED LONDON NEWS

HIGH WATER                    SPRING TIDES.

LOW D.º

NEW LIGHTHOUSE ON BISHOP ROCK, SCILLY ISLANDS.

such dangerous seas, was a major feat of engineering and a great tribute to Walker, the Douglasses and to the workmen who toiled in extremely uncomfortable and, sometimes, terrifying conditions. It is amazing that no loss of life occurred in the face of so many potential hazards and in such a notorious location. The congratulations received from the various bodies were more than well deserved.

In all, the lighthouse had been constructed of 35,209 cubic feet of granite, weighing 2,708 tons.[46]

FINISHING OFF

Later in September 1858 Capts Weller and Redman met with Augustus Smith to discuss their occupation of Rat Island, and the three reached a settlement. A letter was subsequently written to Smith about the surrender of premises, saying the work was nearly finished and they were prepared 'to vacate the entire premises on or before 1st November next ensuing, excepting the Carpenter's Shop above the Store Room in the Yard, to which there is an entrance outside, and the Saw Pit which it is proposed to retain as long as they may be required for the Completion of the Light Keepers Cottages. They also propose to leave the Crane on the Pier and the Tramway leading to it as belonging to you, and to pay for the use of the premises a rent of £20 p.ann. commencing from 1st January 1851, and terminating 31st Dec. next'.[47] Trinity House expressed the hope that the terms would be acceptable and luckily, in due course, Smith wrote concurring with the terms for his property and was paid £160 rent.

Unfortunately, the 'entire premises' on the pier were not vacated by 1 November. This gave Augustus Smith more cause for complaint, which he did on 24 December. As a result, Trinity House told Nicholas Douglass to vacate them by 15 January 1859, and to remove the wooden building used as an office, and make good the fence on the site.[48]

But on 3 January 1859 Douglass informed them that he could not vacate the Carpenter's Shop until March as the dwellings were not ready. He had not been able to fit the dry fittings as the weather had been too wet. He suggested Smith should be paid a moderate rent for the workshop. Smith's response was not recorded.

In mid-September 1858 the Light Committee and William Douglass inspected the lighthouse, reached by steps cut into the granite rock which led to the metal dog-steps fixed to the tower up to the door. The structure met with their approval, especially as the green of the lantern was not as apparent as feared. Three men were still working there, finishing off small jobs, and two men were preparing for delivery of the stove. They then sailed for St Mary's and inspected the progress of the keepers' houses. The walls of two were up, and William Douglass expressed the hope that all four would be completed in January 1859. On their departure, the

Committee compared the lighthouse with that of St Agnes and concluded that the latter burned brighter; they lost sight of Bishop Rock at ten miles and St Agnes at 16 miles.

Supplies of oil and water were to be regularly taken to Bishop Rock. Taking advantage of such a trip, Augustus Smith and some of his friends boarded Trinity House's vessel *Irene* to visit the lighthouse. At this stage, reliefs of the lighthouse keepers and supply trips were undertaken from Tresco by the same relief crew for the Seven Stones light vessel.

To commemorate the building of Bishop Rock lighthouse, Walker was ordered to design an inscription plate to be put up inside the building.

London silversmiths, Edward Barnard & Sons, also decided to commemorate the occasion in 1858 by crafting an exact replica of the lighthouse in silver. This came up for auction in 1974 and was bought by Trinity House for the sum of £1,900.

## SPECIFICATIONS OF THE 1858 LIGHTHOUSE

Height of Tower: 147 feet
Height of Light above MHW: 110 feet
Light Source: Argand lamps
Character: Fixed white
Candle Power: 15,000
Range of Light: 16 miles
Fog Warning Apparatus: 5 hundredweight bell (fixed in 1859)
Cost: £34,599 18s 9d

*Reliefs during bad weather.* ILLUSTRATED LONDON NEWS

CHAPTER FOUR

# 1859 TO 1873

## TOLLS

The issue of light dues or tolls, payable by passing vessels, had been rumbling on between Trinity House and the Board of Trade for some time, and it is pertinent to say something about this here.

At a Royal Commission of 1861:

> The Elder Brethren were of the opinion that there should not be any toll for this light, in consideration of its having been commenced before the passing of the Merchant Shipping Act, 1854, and of the trade not having invited its erection nor pledged themselves to contribute; the work having been regarded as an adjunct to the Scilly Light (St Agnes lighthouse), the tolls for which are sufficient to maintain both.[1]

However, the Board of Trade persisted and, on 20 April 1859, their official notification was sent to Trinity House stating that tolls were to be levied for Bishop Rock lighthouse of one farthing per ton on overseas vessels and 6d per vessel on coasters. Circulars to this effect were to be sent to the toll collectors, giving instructions under what circumstances tolls were to be charged and the voyages to which they applied.

Trinity House expressed regret but had no option but to comply, and gave an order that tolls were now required:[2]

> Upon all Vessels that now pay a Toll for the St Agnes Lighthouse, excepting those crossing a supposed line drawn from the Lands End to Ushant and navigating between the Lands End and the Scilly Islands and vice versa, and excepting also vessels navigating to or from the Scilly Islands to or from ports in the United Kingdom Eastward of a supposed line drawn from Carnsore Point on the S.E. Coast of Ireland to the Bishop Rock Light House.

These new tolls were not well received by masters of shipping. In July 1859, Mr Richardson, a toll collector on Scilly, reported difficulties in collecting light dues from vessels calling in with goods and supplies. They anchored in the Roadstead, a considerable distance from shore, and refused to pay. He asked for additional notices to distribute to the parties concerned.

## DEATH AVERTED

A tragedy was averted on the lighthouse when, in January 1859, one of the keepers nearly drowned while 'dipping' salt water with a bucket. Although not named in Trinity House records, this was probably Assistant Keeper John Williams. There is a family tradition, passed down through the generations to the present day, that he narrowly escaped drowning while on the lighthouse. Having fallen into the sea, he could not be found by the other keepers. But then a slick of blood was sighted, and he was consequently located and pulled to safety. As a result of the accident, Trinity House ordered the fitting of a salt water pump, only to overturn this decision shortly afterwards. To install the pump, Nicholas Douglass would have needed special instructions from Walker as he would have had to cut a groove ten inches below low water, and this might have interfered with some of the joggles (joints) in the stonework; a pipe placed outside would not have withstood a single gale. Also, cisterns were provided in the tower for 2,800 gallons of water 'and if filled when opportunity occurs, would render it impossible they could ever require water'.[3]

By February, the new dwellings on St Mary's had been slated in and prepared for plastering, and the gardens were nearly walled in, so Mr Cooper was instructed to affix the Corporation's Arms to the houses, where they can be seen today.

Also this month, the fog bell and its machinery were delivered to Douglass for the lighthouse and were duly fitted. The bell was worked by a clockwork mechanism and had to be kept wound up during foggy weather by the relevant keeper on duty.

## ROYAL COMMISSION REPORT 1861

Both the 1861 Royal Commission Report into Lights Buoys and Beacons, and Trinity House records discuss the trip to Bishop Rock lighthouse on 8 July 1859 made by the Light Commissioners. They described it as magnificent, with the light 'first order and a beautiful work'. However, not all was good. They found that the lantern panes leaked considerably and the lantern ironwork was rusty, both needing repairs. Also, the keepers complained that the wicks were too small for the burners.

The Principal Keeper, who had worked on both the Eddystone and Longships, thought that the sea was slightly worse at Bishop Rock, with spray going over the top at 110 feet.

But overall, the Commissioners were struck by the superiority of the building in respect of its design, materials, workmanship, finish and internal arrangements. The light was tested at 1am the following morning and consequently described as 'a beautiful "sharp" light'.

Of the fog bell they were not so complimentary. They found that they could scarcely hear it when it was sounded a quarter of a mile away even when their vessel, *Vivid*, which was to windward in a slight breeze, was halted at sea. It was thought to be inefficient owing to some mistake in fixing it. The issue of audibility was not resolved for decades.

It is from this report we learn that, initially, the lighthouse was painted white and not red as had been first mooted back in the 1840s. This paint had virtually peeled off already, to reveal the grey granite beneath, which the Commissioners felt was the worst possible colour for being seen at sea. However, Hugh Tregarthen informed them that the keepers' eyes were affected by the glare when painted white.

*Assistant Keeper John Williams, in Trinity House uniform.*
COURTESY
GREG HOPKINS

The keepers were also suffering from mild scurvy. Vegetables would not keep for long and, consequently, the medicine chest was often visited! (Standard medicine chests were provided for all lighthouses in England and Scotland.) They recommended that keepers at rock lighthouses should be provided with preserved vegetables, lime juice and anti-scorbutics. Writing in 1865, Alphonse Esquiros commented that fresh meat and vegetables would not keep on the lighthouse so the keepers 'are at times attacked by scurvey'.[4]

Circular No. III, issued by Trinity House and published in the Royal Commission Report of 1861, gives some interesting information about the lighthouse at this time. The height of the lighthouse from base to

weather vane was 147ft, the height of the light above the spring water tides was 110ft, and the distance of sea horizon from the light was 11¹/₆ miles. It also reveals that the lighthouse had a flagstaff.

The tower was entirely solid to 45 feet above high water. Above this solid base the wall was four feet nine inches thick, while at the top it had tapered to two feet.

The light was non-revolving, and the apparatus was dioptric with eight reflectors of eight to the circle, with 19 zones of prisms, 13 above and six below the refractor; there was a four concentric wick lamp, with a regulating condenser. The mode of ventilation was by Faraday's tube, four and a half inches diameter over the frame of the lamp, and by openings in the lantern murette or pedestal.

The diameter of the lantern was 14 feet, and its height was: murette five feet; glass 10 feet three inches; glass to vane 12 feet nine inches; (total 28 feet). Its final cost, including the fitting of it, was £1,452 1s.

The cost of the illuminating apparatus, including fittings and cost of transport, was £1,313 10s.

For the four months Bishop Rock lighthouse was operational in 1858, it used 190 gallons of oil, and 12 yards of wick. The wick was made from concentric cotton at 7 ¹/₂d per yard, and cost 7s 6d in 1858.

The price of the fog signal apparatus was £244 15s.

Five spare lamps (the hollow wick oil lamps) were kept together with one reservoir and one receiver. Oil was stored on the first floor in containers in the storeroom. This room measured 12 feet six inches in diameter, eight feet 11 inches in height. There was a barometer with thermometer attached, and an external and internal thermometer.

Three of the keepers were constantly on the lighthouse and one on shore in rotation. They were relieved by a sailing tender with the assistance, when necessary, of a hired boat's crew.

The Principal Keeper was paid £53 p.a. and the Assistant Keepers £43 10s p.a. 1s 6d a day was allowed for victualling, a suit of clothes was issued annually, and coal, oil and furniture for the dwellings were provided. The combined cost of the completed lighthouse and cottages was £36,559 18s 9d.

On 16 August, following the Commissioners' visit, a replacement fog bell of nine hundredweight, costing £367 16s 8d was approved for the lighthouse and was to be made by Wilkins & Co. But later in the month, it was decided that a larger fog bell was needed so the approval was put on hold. The matter was considered again on 25 October and, although no conclusions were recorded, events in early 1860 were to make a decision vital.

Lightning conductors were fitted on all English lighthouses as standard, so Bishop Rock had one installed as a matter of course.

The keepers' cottages had been finished by September, and the Light Committee recommended that deductions be made from the keepers' wages as they were now provided with residences, which had a good supply of spring water. The cost of the dwellings was £2,100, which included a 1,100 feet stone boundary wall. Assistant Keeper Henry Williams married Joyce Hicks of St Mary's in April 1860, so he was one of the first keepers to occupy one of these houses.

*Former Lighthouse Keepers' dwellings today.*
ELISABETH STANBROOK

## THE 1860 STORM

In early February 1860 Hugh Tregarthen wrote to Trinity House informing them that the five hundredweight fog bell at Bishop Rock lighthouse had broken off during the tempestuous weather of Monday 30 January. A westerly to west-north-westerly gale had blown in from 9am onwards, and a signal for assistance was seen flying from the lighthouse.

The *Cornish Telegraph* told of 'tornado-like' gusts of wind and a 'gale of awful violence'. They further reported that windows of plate glass, $^5/_8$ inch thick had been broken in and the lighthouse was flooded. The structure had shaken so much during the storm that earthenware from the men's cupboards was thrown down. Also, the brass entrance door, which had cost £300, had been swept away. On the Wednesday following the storm, Mr Davies of St Agnes had gone out to Bishop Rock but was unable to communicate satisfactorily with the keepers. However, a bag with a letter from them 'was drawn off to the boat' by ropes, giving details of what had occurred. *The Exeter Flying Post* somehow calculated that £1,000 worth of damage had been done. It was not until the Saturday that Hugh Tregarthen managed to land on Bishop Rock to see for himself.

Although the lighthouse was damaged during the storm, the newspaper report appears to have sensationalised the event. Hugh Tregarthen informed Trinity House that the crane had remained intact but 'the Ladder and Flag Pole which were lashed on the Gallery Rail are broken by the Force of the Sea and the Dome of the Lens is cracked in several places in the way of the Brass fastenings'.[5] But the building itself was found to be perfectly secure, and he felt the damage to the apparatus was of little consequence, although he suggested more stays could be considered.

*Trinity House Corporation's emblem.*
ELISABETH STANBROOK

William Douglass went out to make an inspection on 15 February, and confirmed that the damage was unimportant. Writing of this later in the *Proceedings of the Institution of Civil Engineers*,[6] Nicholas Douglass's grandson William Tregarthen Douglass, said how a portion of the fog bell was found in a cleft of the rock and was preserved at Trinity House. This was found by the keepers who, 'with difficulty and risk' recovered it together with some other pieces.[7] For this, Trinity House decided to award them with a present of half a guinea each. It would seem that a steel bell was installed shortly afterwards.

Interestingly, below the rock in recent years, divers have found what might be the remains of a bell, with the top part missing, and they speculate whether this might be the remains of the one lost.[8]

An inspection by Trinity House at the lighthouse five months later in July 1860 found 'everything beautifully clean and in good order'.[9] But nothing had been done to alter the supports to the lens. They found the cementing of glass in the lantern to be cracked and defective in various places, and water found its way down in considerable quantities into the Watch Room ...'this should be remedied forthwith and holes drilled in the corrugated iron lining to admit air'.

At 3.30pm that afternoon they landed on St Mary's and inspected the keepers' dwellings which they also found clean and in good order. The Committee recommended that each house should have a small outhouse for storing potatoes and wood etc, and a drain of rounded tiles at the edge of the garden slopes to take the water off the gravel paths.

After this, they sailed for New Grimsby, Tresco, and landed the annual supplies of stores for Bishop Rock and Seven Stones. The following day, they visited the Tresco houses where the crew of the Seven Stones light vessel lived, accompanied by Tregarthen, their affairs for Bishop Rock completed.

It may have been due to the severity of the 1860 storm that a device was fitted to the lighthouse for measuring waves that winter.[10]

In 1862 Hugh Tregarthen reported that the crew of the Seven Stones light vessel had asked to be relieved from the danger and risk involved in conveying coals and water to Bishop Rock from 'Great' Grimsby. He suggested the reliefs could be effected from St Agnes as, from here, the distance to Bishop Rock was only four miles while from 'Great' Grimsby it was eight. From St Agnes, the total cost per annum would be £50.

Trinity House approved this, and so began a new phase of reliefs. They were carried out by Mr Obadiah Hicks of St Agnes in his gig *O & M*, the initials representing his first name and that of his wife, Mary.

The Committee visited the keepers' houses in July 1863, and found them in 'beautiful order', having been lately painted. But not all was well with the inhabitants. The Principal Keeper, Mr Watson, found spending so much time confined in the lighthouse very stressful and detrimental to his health, and he asked to be moved to a shore-based one. Trinity House told him to get a medical certificate so that they could consider his request. Tregarthen spoke highly of him saying that he kept the apparatus in good order, and the Visiting Committee said he had 'a very high character, and that he possesses a considerable amount of mechanical skill which might make him a useful servant at such stations as Gibraltar'.[11] His case was treated as exceptional and he was allowed to leave. On the recommendation of the Light Committee, it was agreed to promote Assistant Keeper John Williams to Principal Keeper, and to replace him with Francis Ellis.

The Committee visited Bishop Rock again in September and, as usual, found all in good order. But they did recommend a new lamp of the best construction to be placed there and a gun metal bell in place of the steel one which they condemned as a failure. They then went to St Mary's where their vessel was being lengthened by seven feet to cope with the work.

Eleven months after the new lamp was first suggested, it was decided that Chance Brothers & Co, of Birmingham, would undertake an adjustment to the lens at Bishop Rock for £120, together with an extra sum for the wages of the mechanics during their detainment on Scilly, or the lighthouse, because of the weather.

## TROUBLE WITH AUGUSTUS SMITH

A snippet of information volunteered by Hugh Tregarthen in January 1863 revealed that relations between Augustus Smith and Trinity House had changed considerably (meaning unfavourably!) within the last year. No details were given but this seemed to be the way of things between them from now on. It is well documented that Smith disapproved of Trinity House using young men as lighthouse keepers. He favoured employing older, more experienced men who had been pilots or mariners, and who knew the sea well.

In late March 1865 the Duchy of Cornwall wrote saying that an arrangement had been made whereby Augustus Smith, 'the resident Lord Farmer of the Islands' would be entitled from last Michaelmas to the rent of £10 a year for the St Mary's dwellings, payable by Trinity House under the lease of 12 June 1858, the Duchy still retaining another rent of £20.

Settlement was required of £29 3s 9d. This was paid.

Ten months later, in January 1866, conflict between Trinity House and Augustus Smith broke out again. Smith had proposed to introduce a road rate and impose this charge on the keepers who 'cut up' the roads when carting seaweed from the beaches to their gardens in which they grew early vegetables for sale. The Corporation's solicitors wrote to him pointing out that they were exempt from all rates and taxes, and the payment of this was intended to be optional by the keepers.

The following month, Hugh Tregarthen informed Trinity House that no warning about the road rate had been given by the overseers but, on examining the Rate Book, he found the road rate inserted in Augustus Smith's handwriting. Smith then claimed that it was never intended for the keepers' payment of the rate to be optional, and he had subsequently prevented them from taking the seaweed while they chose not to pay it.

The saga continued into March, when Tregarthen wrote again, saying that Smith had forbidden his tenants to use the roads in any way for the 'Establishment', i.e. Trinity House. It was only when Tregarthen offered to pay the rate that Smith rescinded the order. Had this not happened, 'not one of his Tenants would have taken a tin of Oil to the Light House'[12] when the yacht came in with the annual supplies. It would seem that Augustus Smith had won that dispute.

The engineer's report of July 1866 revealed that the pointing on the lighthouse was defective, and it was consequently repaired under the direction of Scillonian, Mr Meneer.

KEEPER TROUBLE

Sadly, John Williams' time as Principal Keeper at Bishop Rock was taking its toll. On 5 September:

> It being represented that Williams now Principal Keeper at Bishop Rock Lighthouse is in such a state of health that his residence at the Rock is no longer possible, and that he is desirous of being removed to a shore station; and that the circumstance of his having been appointed Principal before his turn for promotion, because of the Exposed position of the Light House and his volunteering for duty there, being considered: It was Resolved that Williams be removed from Bishop Rock to a Shore Station, and return to the position he would have occupied as an Assistant, had he been moved to shore when made Principal of the Bishop Rock.[13]

Hugh Tregarthen found himself in trouble with Trinity House when the lighthouse keepers signalled that they wanted beef and water. No doubt, having consumed all their fresh provisions, the novelty of dried food was wearing a little thin. Complying with their request, he managed to get provisions to them 'by hauling a line from the Top of the House'. Much displeased with this, Trinity House told him it must not happen again.

Towards the end of October 1866 it was the Bishop Rock lighthouse keepers who found themselves on the wrong side of Trinity House. They had all communicated with each other and then written one united petition to them, delivered by Tregarthen. They claimed that their living costs, such as clothing, provisions and education were increasing and, as a consequence, they wanted higher pay. This did not go down too well. Trinity House considered their pay and 'advantages' they received equal to those of a similar status. Thus no pay rise would be forthcoming. Furthermore, the keepers were informed that if Trinity House found that any attempt had been made stir up discontent in the service, it would be met with the punishment it deserved.

Hugh Tregarthen suggested in April 1867 that fresh provisions in tins should be kept at Bishop Rock for reserve instead of salt meat, and also at other rock stations. This was approved.

It was as early as November 1867 that a plan to enlarge and heighten the lighthouse was drawn up by James Douglass, but this was not put into effect until the 1880s, as seen below.

The Light Committee recommended in December 1868 the addition of a Supernumerary Assistant Keeper (SAK) to the staff at Bishop Rock as an experiment during winter months. Reliefs of alternate months were, they felt, starting to affect the health of the keepers as there was nowhere that they could take exercise in the fresh air or, indeed, in the lighthouse itself.

However, the idea of an increase in staff was eventually scrapped. Instead they recommended that an extra boat hire be allowed to effect the relief every three weeks during the winter months.

In January 1869 Hugh Tregarthen told the Committee that extra duties by the St Agnes Principal Keeper involved the taking charge of oil and stores for Bishop Rock. He was to be paid £5 p.a. allowance for this and other duties that might be required.

In April Tregarthen sent Trinity House a letter from the keepers together with their medical certificates regarding their state of health. The men were to be relieved and allowed to come ashore, but no details of these ailments were given. In May, AK Francis Ellis, sent Trinity House a petition for his removal from the lighthouse, plus a medical certificate, and he went to London. July found him at the Corporation's Buoy Wharf, while his application to work on a shore lighthouse was considered.

The Committee went out to the lighthouse in early summer 1869 and found the lens needed repairing with putty, and both the winch and WC were out of order. William Douglass was told to attend to these matters and, in July, it was decided to send Chance Brothers & Co out to effect repairs.

On 7 September Trinity House approved the recommendation by Douglass to raise the Bishop Rock light apparatus by about $1\frac{1}{2}$ inches with a view to preventing the interruption of light by the horizontal bars of the lantern. He was requested to do it soon so that the mechanics working on the Wolf Rock light could be used. However, it appears this was deferred until 1871 when, on 18 September, Douglass visited Bishop Rock lighthouse and consequently submitted an estimate of £45 for this work to be carried out. It was not until a year later that William Douglass visited the lighthouse and adjusted the apparatus.

In early February 1873 the Light Committee reported, 'There is an over-lapping ledge at the landing place of the Bishop which the Committee recommend should be chipped away and two foot holds made for the convenience of landing at dead low water'.[14] Instructions were sent to the engineer to undertake this. But by July, it had not been done and Trinity House became increasingly concerned as it 'frequently catches the nose of the landing boat and should be removed before some fatal accident happens'.

In July the Committee reported that the Wesleyan Chapel in Garrison Lane, St Mary's was in a dilapidated condition. It is from this we learn that the lighthouse keepers attended the chapel in preference to any other place of worship. As a consequence, Trinity House decided to make a donation towards its repair.

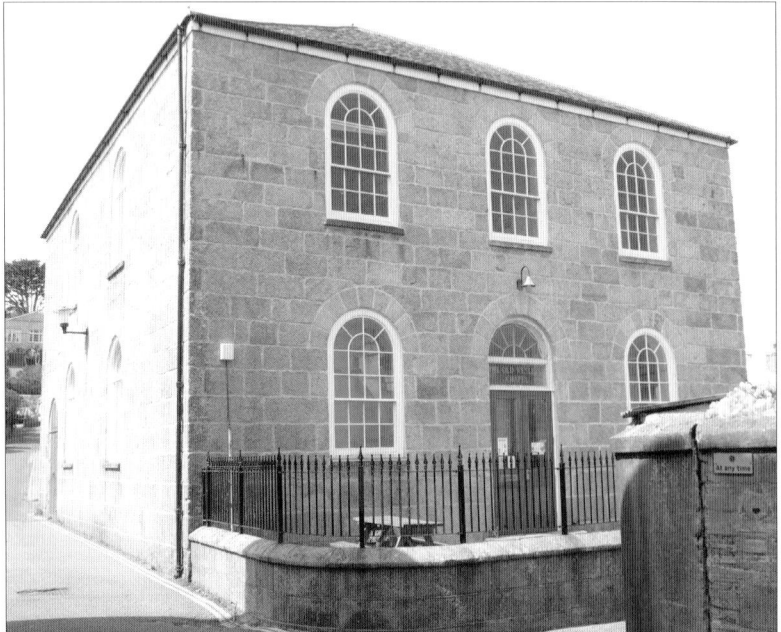

*The former Wesleyan Chapel today.*
ELISABETH STANBROOK

# CHAPTER FIVE

# 1874 TO 1881

Ownership of the Duchy of Cornwall lease for the Isles of Scilly had changed hands upon the death of Augustus Smith on 31 July 1872, passing to his nephew Mr Dorrien Smith. Nearly five years later, on 15 March 1877, Dorrien Smith's solicitor wrote to Trinity House requesting information about their rents payable to him for pieces of land on St Mary's and St Agnes. On the advice of their own solicitors, Trinity House informed him that they paid the Duchy of Cornwall £20 rent for St Agnes, and Dorrien Smith, the lessee, £10 for the dwellings on St Mary's.

## STORM NECESSITATES STRENGTHENING

A terrific storm from the north-west hit the Isles of Scilly on Monday 13 April 1874, and the lighthouse was exposed to the full fury of the elements. This must have been a truly terrifying experience for the keepers who could only have watched helplessly as waves passed their kitchen window at a height of 70 feet or more. Occasional waves broke over the lantern causing the light reflected from the lens to be thrown back again producing a blaze of light within the lighthouse. The noise, too, must have been tremendous, adding to the trauma of the event. AK Upton was relieved two days after the storm, and he 'looked as if the trying ordeal through which he had so lately passed had anything but a beneficial effect on him'.[1]

Tregarthen wrote immediately to Trinity House informing them of the storm and that the sea had struck the lantern cracking the lens (the prisms of the apparatus) and the lantern glass in places. However, he followed this letter with a telegram on 20 April saying his son had visited the lighthouse and found the damage 'was not so much as reported calling attention to the exaggeration in a local newspaper'.[2]

Indeed, *The Cornish Telegraph* carried a dramatic report:

> ... a sea struck the house with such force as to start two panes in the lantern and crack and splinter the Fresnel lens in from 20 to 30 places...The light-keepers say it appeared as if a cannon had struck

the house! For a moment all was still, and the house vibrated and shook so that the things fell from their places; the putty etc from the fittings of the lens began to fall about their heads; and they had to hold on to anything they could reach.

Less than half an hour later, it reported, the sea struck the lighthouse again with great force.

> … and a tremendous crash followed. This was found to proceed from all the spare cylinders (for the light) in the service-room being thrown down and broken, two only being left. These were for safety rolled in flannel and put one in the bed-place and the other in a pail, for without a cylinder they could not keep a light.

The newspaper also reported that the cement in the joints of the lighthouse was coming away with the result that the structure was 'leaking', and that the power of the huge seas was such that sand was carried up from the sea bed in the great waves into the gallery.

The Editor of the newspaper *Engineer* later picked up on this report and wrote to Trinity House in June for further details, and was told that what had appeared in print did not possess any scientific quality!

Douglass was instructed to visit the lighthouse to assess the damage for himself and then take the necessary measures. Due to the damage that was caused by the hurricane winds, which included tower vibrations and the splitting of external granite blocks a few feet above high water, Douglass recommended strengthening the tower from top to bottom by 'bolting heavy iron ties to the internal surface of the walls, connecting them through the floors'.[3] He obtained estimates for the work required and, in July, he sent his report as to the best mode of undertaking this, with an estimated cost of £2,350. The work took place, but even these measures were to prove insufficient against the might of the sea.

### THE SCHILLER

A major incident with tragic consequences occurred on the Isles of Scilly on 7 May 1875 when the German-built *Schiller*, a 3,600 ton steamer en route from New York to Plymouth, struck the Retarrier Ledges and foundered with huge loss of life. Thick fog and strong currents had caused the vessel to go off-course, and only 53 out of 364 people on board survived. In the lighthouse, the keepers and Thomas Cole from Penzance, who was there to undertake repairs, were painfully aware of the tragedy unfolding but were powerless to help. They must have been absolutely devastated not to have been able to afford any assistance to those in the perilous grip of weather and tides. One of the keepers was observed coming outside and holding out a green light, but to no avail. Their

*The SCHILLER before her fateful journey.*
ILLUSTRATED
LONDON NEWS

horror is reflected in a moving and poignant letter the senior keeper on duty wrote to his wife:

> With heart-sick grief I write this to inform you of the dreadful wreck that has happened here, less than a half-mile inside of us, on Friday night, the 7th inst. I had the watch up to eight pm, when the man who is doing duty here during the absence of a principal keeper took on, but seeing a thick fog coming on I still kept in the lantern, and ordered the bell to be set going at 8.40pm – fog very thick. I timed the bell properly at six strokes per minute, and saw that all was right. I left the lantern at 10pm, and went to my bunk, but I could not sleep.
>
> At 11.35pm, William Mortimer came running down and called to me, and said he could see a vessel on the rocks. I jumped up and went out on the parapet without stopping to dress, and saw the masthead and starboard light of a large steamer. She was burning blue lights and firing off guns and rockets. She seemed to be sinking. The last gun was fired at 1.30 on the 8th inst. I relieved G. Gould at four am.
>
> Fog again raised at six am, and I could then just see the topmast of the vessel out of the water. We could count about 26 people in the rigging. I could see one lady in the lee side of the rigging with two males by her. She was in a sitting posture, I should think lashed. It was a dreadful sight. At about seven am the

mast fell, and I supposed every one perished, but I still hope a few or some might have been saved.

On Sunday three bodies floated past us, and this afternoon more have passed close to us. No one knows what was felt in this house by all hands to see so many of our dear fellow-creatures suffering and dying so near to us. Their sufferings must have been severe, for it was a cold drizzling rain all night, wind W.S.W. I think you had better take this letter, together with my compliments, to Mr John Banfield, Lloyd's agent.

I remain, your affectionate husband,

JAMES DANIEL.

Relief contractor Obadiah Hicks, and a quickly assembled crew in the *O & M*, rowed out through the Western Rocks and rescued four survivors. Other boats managed to rescue a few others but the majority of those on board perished in the treacherous seas.

By 10 May, the bodies of 24 men and 17 women had been placed in 'a cellar by the pier'[4] on St Mary's, representing just a few of those victims who would be found over the next few days.

Later that month, and, after due consideration, Tregarthen decided it was not necessary to mark the wreck of the *Schiller*, and he sent extracts from the Bishop Rock lighthouse log book to Trinity House for them to read:

> Observed during short rise of fog at 11.30pm a Vessel on the Rocks between here and Rosevear burning blue lights. Rockets and Guns firing Fog Bell going from 8.40pm to 11.30 pm, again from 11.45pm to 8th instant 8.40am. Observed at 6.20am short rise of fog the masts of a Vessel standing in sea. Crew in the rigging. Masts went by board at about 7am, nothing but floating wreck when fog cleared'.[5]

The helplessness of the lighthouse keepers hit a chord with the Scilly Coroner and he wrote to Trinity House suggesting that a means of telegraphic communication should be fitted at the lighthouse (their response was not recorded, but the suggestion was declined). Had this been installed before the event, it was felt that sufficient boats could have been launched to save all passengers and crew. This sentiment was echoed by Francis Banfield & Sons, Agents to Lloyds. However, James Douglass said that this method of telecommunication was not really possible at the

*One of two* SCHILLER *signal guns at Valhalla Museum, Tresco.*
ELISABETH
STANBROOK

lighthouse due to the weather and the force of the sea. The wear and tear to the cable against the granite rock would be enormous.

The following July, the Board of Trade asked Trinity House on the advisability of supplying Bishop Rock lighthouse and a few others with some 'call rockets' for use in emergencies. This they considered advisable, and recommended that rock-based lighthouses, including Bishop Rock, should have one dozen maroon rockets of the corporate pattern in a copper case. Thus the keepers, at last, had some means of communication with the inhabited islands.

## FOG SIGNAL

The ineffectiveness of the fog bell must have been foremost in people's minds during this time. To be caught out in the Western Rocks in thick fog, before the introduction of technological innovations used today, would have been any mariner's nightmare. But it was to be several years before anything was done to upgrade the equipment.

At the Board of Trade Inquiry into the loss of the *Schiller* in June 1875, James Douglass said he felt the fog signal could not be improved upon at the lighthouse, and suggested one could be fitted on Crebawethan, an island to the north-east. This was never done.

In July 1877 Dorrien Smith asked if fog signal rockets could be used at Bishop Rock lighthouse, but Trinity House said they were at an experimental stage only. Four years later, they did introduce rockets for use in thick fog, which were to be adopted at 15 minute intervals, while double rockets were in the process of being tested. The estimated expenditure for the storage and firing of these rockets was £90. In late October, having tested the double rockets, it was decided that single rockets only were to be discharged, and at 10 minute intervals. However, the fog bell was to remain.

## THE LIGHT

In the meantime, Douglass had successfully recommended a 6-wick Trinity House Douglass burner for Bishop Rock to replace the original 4-wick Fresnel burner. It was ordered from DeVille & Co at £13 4s. In September 1875 he also recommended that a pressure lamp be placed in the lighthouse in place of the existing hydrostatic lamp - it offered greater facilities for repair, as had been found on other rock lighthouses. Trinity House approved this and awarded the scheme £170. They also provided £120 for ventilating valves in the lantern in 1877.

Opposite: *A composite photograph of a storm at Bishop Rock lighthouse.*
C. J. KING & SON

Bishop Rock
Lighthouse in a
howling gale.
Composite photo:
C.J. King & Son, Scilly.
E 35.

MAINTENANCE

Another cracked stone, this time in the 18th course, was discovered at the lighthouse by James Douglass in July 1877. He visited Bishop Rock again on 4 September and concluded it had been caused by a blow from some floating body. £140 was spent in repairs.

Only 18 months later, in early January 1879, Tregarthen wrote to say that another stone at the base of the Bishop Rock tower had cracked. Douglass was sent to inspect it and, subsequently, reported that cracks in the tower were due to the tremors which could be remedied at an estimated cost of £450.[6] This remedial work was approved.

But structural problems were to re-occur, showing just how vulnerable this structure was to the force of the sea. After a heavy storm in the winter of 1881, some pieces of granite were split from the face of the exterior blocks a few feet above high water level – some weighing a half hundredweight. In December, having received reports of the damage, and of tremors, James Douglass was sent to make a detailed inspection of the lighthouse, the result of which was to permanently change the appearance and height of Bishop Rock lighthouse.

KEEPERS

Because they had been provided with houses, the Bishop Rock lighthouse keepers had been paid less than some other keepers. But from March 1876, a receipt was obtained from them for the full rate of wages, and the house rent deducted and treated as an item of miscellaneous revenue.

Various keepers left during this time. Samuel Rogers was discharged from Bishop Rock in August 1875 on account of ill health, while keeper James Daniel was discharged from duty in September. He went to London.

In July 1877 AK Thomas J. Nicholson was dismissed the service. He had been lodging away from his keepers house and had been guilty of 'flagrant misconduct'.[7] Unfortunately no details were given of this misconduct. Tregarthen paid his wages to 17 September, but deducted a full quarter's rent for his dwelling on account of the filthy state in which he left it.

Mr Lloyd, the Principal Keeper at the lighthouse also found himself in trouble in April 1881, and Tregarthen was asked to report on what grounds he was suspected of 'intemperance'. His removal from Bishop Rock was deferred in May until an inquiry had taken place.

THE RELIEFS

One of the relief boat crewmen, J. Williams, was given £5 due to injuries he received while landing heavy cases intended for the works going on there in July 1876 (the lighthouse was undergoing painting work). Also that month, it was agreed to replace the mooring buoy.

Relief contractor, Obadiah Hicks, was paid 10s in August 1876 for damage to his boat in landing stores, and £2 for the boat hire. It would seem the relief boat had had to take provisions to the lighthouse on 8 January 1877 in heavy seas and, in April, Trinity House paid the extra claim of £10 for this service.

*Encasing the original lighthouse.* GIBSON ARCHIVE

CHAPTER SIX

# 1882 TO 1888

## BUILDING WORKS

The next few years were to see major changes to Bishop Rock lighthouse. In early May 1882 Trinity House discussed James Douglass's inspection report, mentioned above, concerning the defective condition of the tower. They decided the time had come to strengthen and improve the tower, both inside and out, and to increase the height by 40 feet.

To achieve this, the old lighthouse was to be encased in an outer skin of granite up to the service-room level, from which point the old structure would be demolished and four new rooms would be added. A new south-facing entrance door was to be made to replace the east-facing one. The foundations would be greatly strengthened by new blocks of granite, dovetailed horizontally and vertically and held in place by iron bolts. This additional stone would add 41,860 cubic feet of granite, weighing an estimated 3,220 tons, to the structure.

The illuminating apparatus and fog signal were to be improved too, and throughout the alterations a temporary light was to be maintained. The height of the mean focal plane of the light above high water of ordinary spring-tides would be increased from 110 feet to 142 feet (as seen on the drawing) and thus the nautical range would be extended from 16 miles to 18 1/4 miles. The estimated cost of the tower reconstruction was, at this stage, £55,000. On a rather lesser scale, Douglass also suggested improving the sanitary arrangements; unfortunately, no details were given describing what the arrangements were, either before or after improvements.

Trinity House proposed establishing another workyard on Rat Island, adjoining the area used for the building of the original lighthouse, and a rent of fifty guineas (£52 10s) p.a. was accepted by Dorrien Smith. Further buildings were erected including overhead travellers, and a railway was laid between the workyard and the steam crane. This crane had been erected on the pier for loading and unloading materials. Plans for this can be seen in the pencil additions to the 1851 plan of the pier (p.42).

Most of the workmen were from the mainland and needed somewhere to live, but resurrecting the now ruinous buildings on Rosevear was not considered. The Admiralty offered the Coastguard premises free of rent on certain conditions (not specified), and the possibility of using the Garrison Barracks was also discussed. The final decision was not recorded.

William Tregarthen Douglass, James's son, was appointed Resident Engineer of the project in June 1882, on a salary of £400 a year. Initially Trinity House and the Board of Trade only wanted to pay him £300 but, finally, the higher sum was accepted. William was later engaged to build the Round Island lighthouse too.

William Douglass had, with his father, worked on the construction of the Eddystone lighthouse (1878 to 1882) and the removal of Smeaton's Tower. He had experienced a narrow escape from death which must have been a terrifying moment, and provides a good example of the perils of building a rock lighthouse:

> Mr W. T. Douglass, a son of the chief engineer, was superintending the lowering of some portion of the upper part when the giving way of the gear hurled him from the top, and he escaped destruction on the exposed rock below only by the opportune inflow of a great wave. Happily he sustained no serious injury'.[1]

Trinity House placed advertisements in *Railway Supplies Journal* and *The Architect* that summer, inviting tenders for supplies of granite. As a result two firms, Robinson & Son (possibly from North Shields) and Shearer & Co, were asked if they would agree to the division of the contract. The former was reluctant and withdrew their tender, but offered to contract for part of the work. The latter also objected to the division, but quoted a price for a supply of granite for the base.

In the end, Trinity House accepted Shearer & Co's tender for granite at a cost of £14,221. Hugh Shearer had taken over the De Lank Quarry near St Breward in 1877, in partnership with Morris Charles Smith, and it operated under the name of Eddystone Granite Company H. Shearer &

*Part of De Lank Quarry today.*
ELISABETH STANBROOK

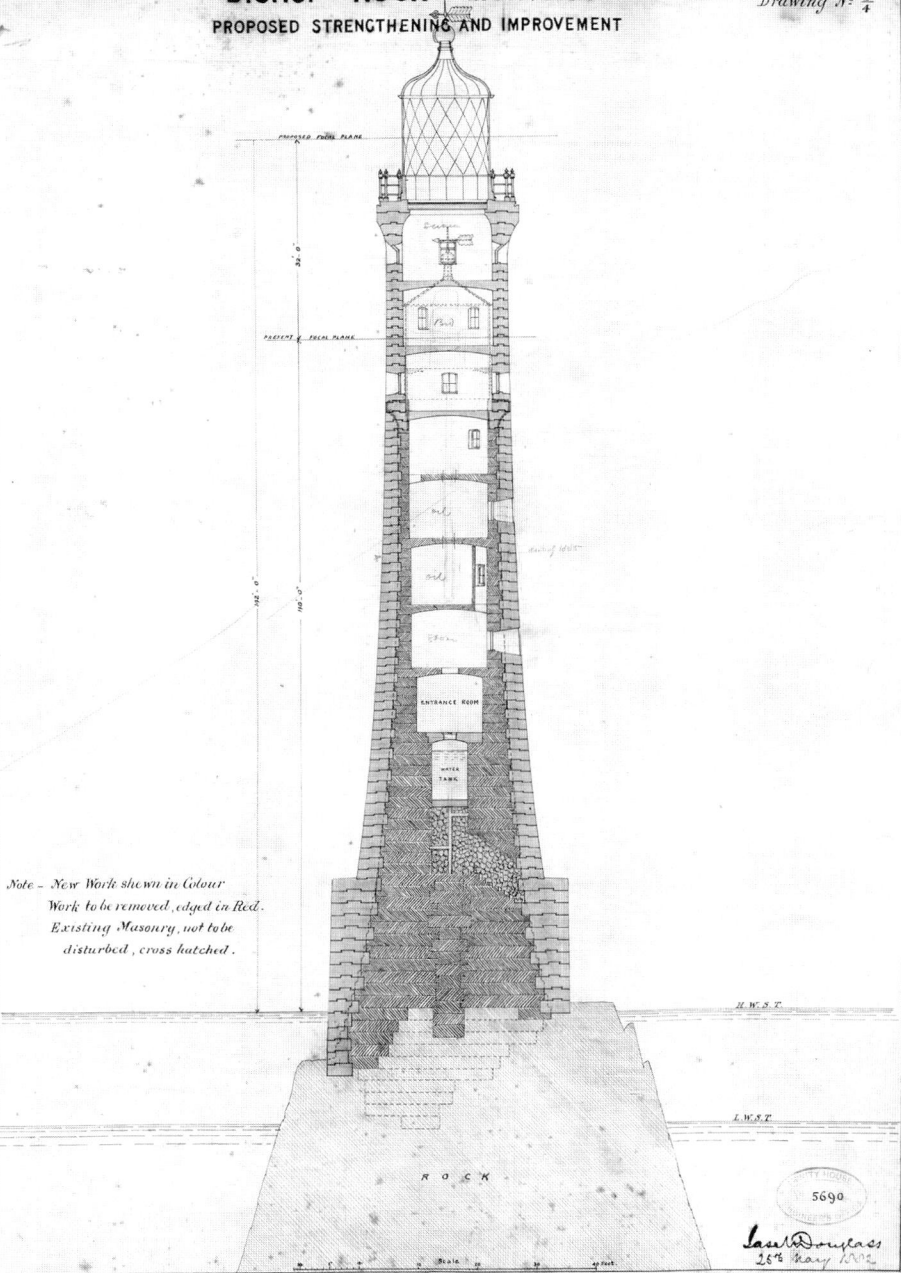

*Plan of proposed strengthening of the tower.* TRINITY HOUSE

Co.[2] They had provided the stone for the Eddystone lighthouse alterations. Shearer put forward Mr T. J. Lindsay as one surety and Wilson & Bromley as the other. The blocks of granite were to be dressed and erected in sections at the quarry before being shipped across to St Mary's. Mr E. Seldon was employed as Inspector of Granite. His main job was to inspect the quarrying and dressing. Mr Joseph Harris, of St Mary's, was made Foreman of the Works on Scilly.

Ensuring supplies of stone on a regular basis was to test Trinity House and Douglass sorely. Shearer & Co had apparently provided excellent materials and workmanship for the alterations to Eddystone lighthouse, and had even completed their contract six months early. So the problems that ensued must have come as an unwelcome surprise for Douglass. By the end of November 1882, there were deep concerns about Shearer & Co's delay in preparing the granite and, by early December, Trinity House decided to consult a solicitor. As a consequence, Shearer & Co were informed that their contract would be transferred unless some progress was made.

In the same month, tenders were invited for the supply of mooring buoys for the 130-ton twin-steamer *Hercules* which had been built on the Clyde in 1870 for James Douglass and his work on the Great and Little Basses lighthouses off Ceylon.[3] On 19 December, Trinity House accepted the tender of Mr Bellamy to supply six moorings for £180.

*Hercules* had also been used in the construction of the Eddystone lighthouse, before being transferred to Scilly for use on Bishop Rock. It had a railway running along its deck to the stern on which a bogie travelled, carrying stone. There were also winches and cranes for manoeuvring the blocks of granite. Mr James was Master of the *Hercules*, and had had his salary increased from £100 to £130 in October.

The increased height and width of the proposed improvements to the tower meant that the maximum attainable width of Bishop Rock itself had to be used as a foundation, amounting to a diametrical base of 41 feet. These size changes would also serve to give additional strength to the structure. The new cylindrical base would be built more or less vertically to a height of 40 feet above the foundation, ending in a landing platform known as the set-off. This was accessible from the rock by a gun-metal ladder or cleats. Upon this set-off would be landed the keepers and stores.

From the set-off, the tower would rise 31 feet in diameter, curving upwards to a cavetto (a concave moulding), upon which the gallery and its lantern would be fixed.

The new 40 feet high cylindrical base meant that a heavy sea crashing against it had less leverage and, therefore, would cause less damage to the foundations below. The wave would divide and be thwarted from travelling upwards much beyond the set-off. It prevented a heavy fall of

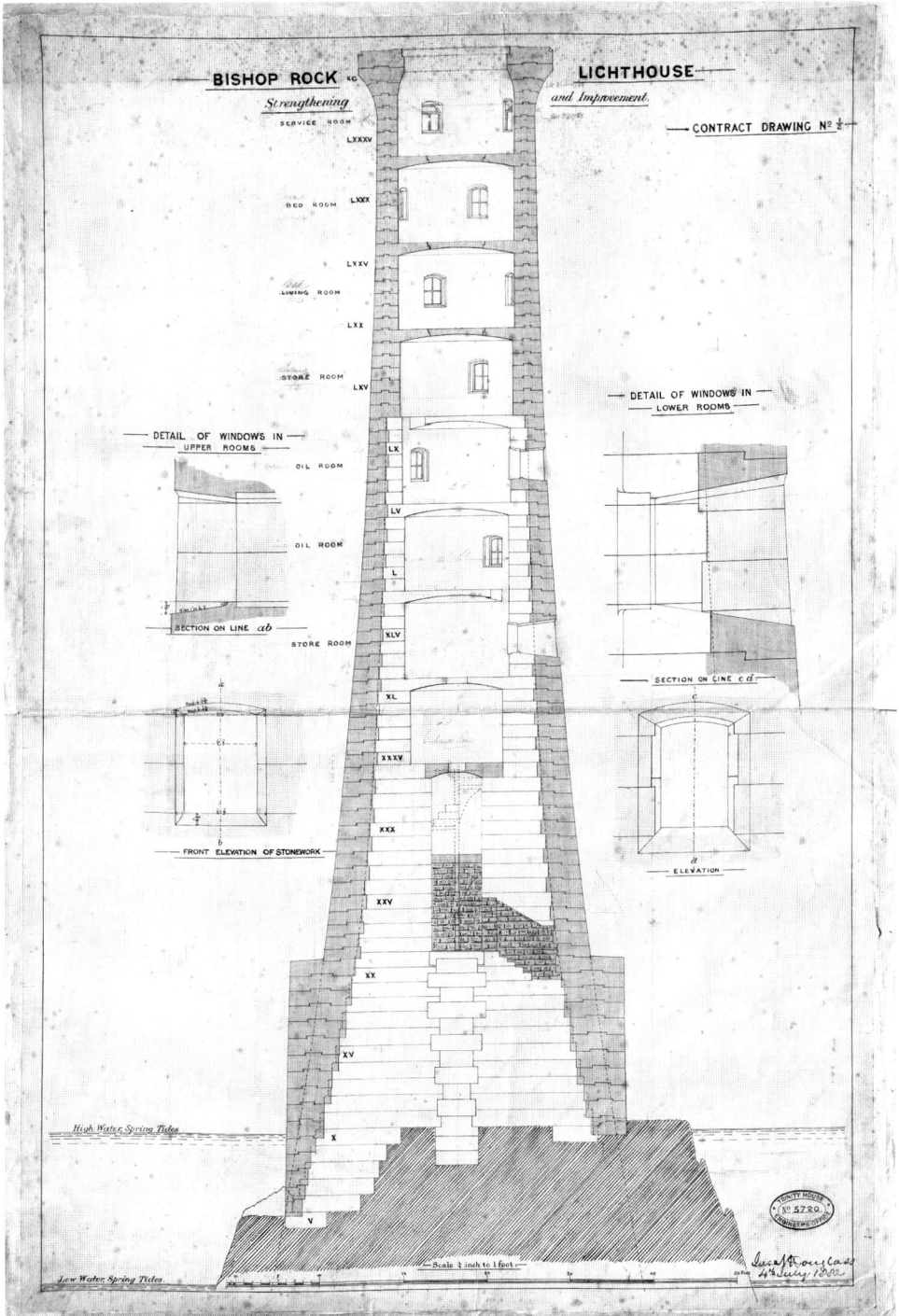

*Proposed strengthening and improvements to the tower.* TRINITY HOUSE

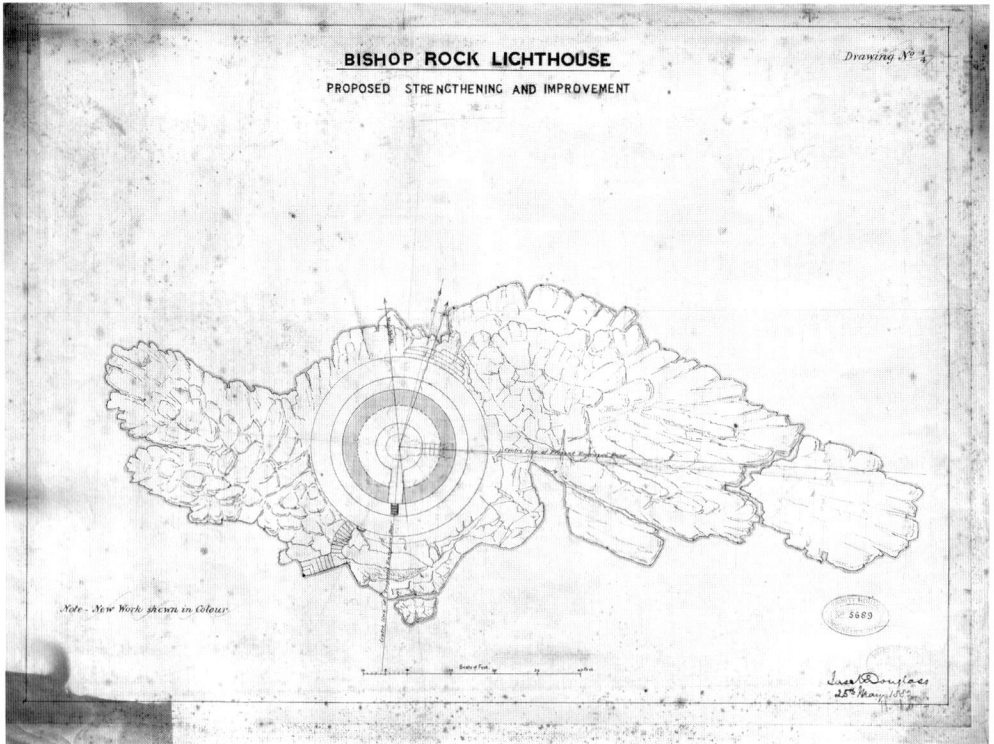

BISHOP ROCK LIGHTHOUSE
PROPOSED STRENGTHENING AND IMPROVEMENT
*Drawing Nº 4*

*Note - New Work shewn in Colour*

*Plan of
strengthening and
improvements of the
tower.*
TRINITY HOUSE

water into the rock.

At the end of January 1883 the tenders were in for the setting crane; Hunter & English were recommended at £355. The tender for supplying yellow metal bolts went to Rogers, Sons & Co.

The year 1883 began badly regarding supplies of granite. Problems caused by Shearer & Co, who were sinking into debt, were continuing apace as the stone did not materialise. Increasingly concerned at this, Trinity House decided that their contract would have to be terminated in early April unless 1,000 cubic feet of granite was delivered to the Corporation's Works before 18 April. This demand was not met, so Trinity House contacted Tamar & Kit Hill Granite Co and Robinson & Son for the immediate supply of seven courses of granite, numbers 10 to 16 inclusive, to meet urgent requirements. Legal steps were then put in hand on 18 April to cancel Shearer & Co's contract.

On 27 April Trinity House accepted Tamar & Kit Hill Co's tender for courses 10, 12 and 14, at 8s 6d per cubic foot, and Robinson & Sons' tender for courses 11, 13, 15 and 16, at 7s 6d per cubic foot.

Just over two weeks later, Shearer & Co actually delivered some granite to the Works. In the meantime, courses eight and nine were ordered from the Tamar & Kit Hill Co, and Shearer & Co were to be informed of this,

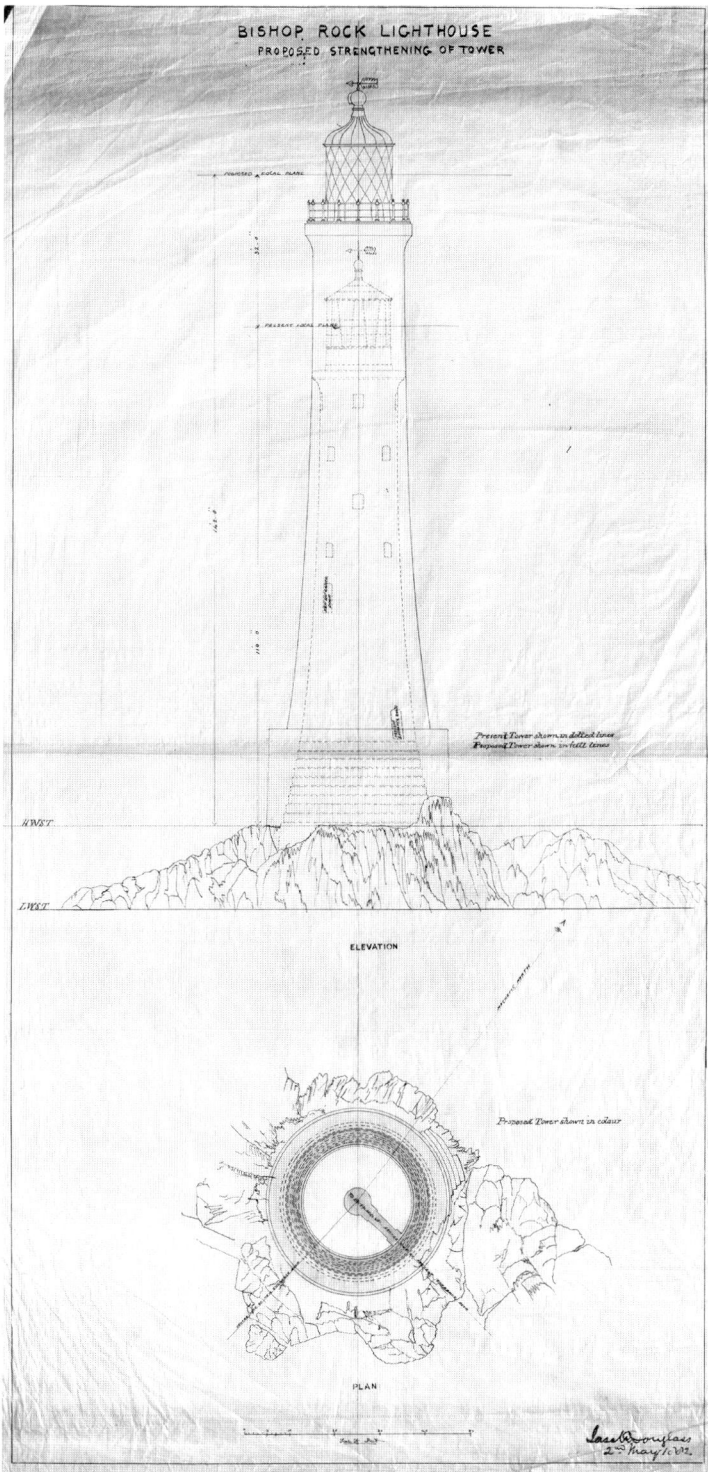

*Elevation of the proposed improvements.*
TRINITY HOUSE

although 11 stones of the eighth course in the hands of Shearer & Co were to be accepted if they were shipped within a week.

While all this was going on, James and William Douglass, together with the workmen, managed a tide's work on 11 April preparing the rock for the foundation of the new masonry, and this work continued until the site was ready. Finally, despite all the problems with supplies of granite, the first stone was laid on 25 May 1883. One of the boatmen who took supplies out for the building work was the father of Capt Stephen (Ste) Jenkins, a future relief contractor and well known Scillonian.

During this early phase of construction, William Douglass explained how each stone up to, and including, course 8 had a male dovetail, six inches in depth at its inner end, to ensure a perfect connection with the granite tower. It was also dovetailed to the other blocks of granite with which it was connected. The average weight of the dovetailed granite blocks was 2 to $3\frac{1}{4}$ tons. They were taken to Bishop Rock by *Hercules* where they were landed on the southern side. Each block was secured to elm rollers in the hold of the vessel.

The workmen, who usually numbered about thirty, were landed on the rock by a manila rope attached to a single-whip winch situated on the gallery of the tower. Their main work here was dressing back the face of the granite rock and cutting out the dovetails. They had to drill holes in the face of the tower into which they inserted steel plugs and feathers. The dovetails were dressed to template by double and single-handed cast steel points. This work was carried out in partnership by a mason and a hammer-man, preparing for each block of new masonry. Within two days on average, they had completed a dovetailed stone, plus one that needed no dovetailing at what would be its inner end.

With continuing problems of granite supplies, Trinity House authorised the placing of advertisements in relevant publications to invite contracts for the remainder of granite necessary to complete Bishop Rock lighthouse. However, this plan was cancelled as Shearer & Co's bankers, Robins, Foster & Co, were willing to advance funds to enable him to finish the contract. Thus, in June 1883, Shearer & Co's contract was renewed on the understanding that the present sureties were maintained.

But the arrival of granite on Scilly continued to be precarious. By November, Robinson & Son were now failing to deliver the stone on time, and Trinity House decided to terminate their contract. Despite this, by the end of the 1883 season, 57 stones, including part of course ten, had been set.

Each stone was bedded and grouted in Portland cement with clean sharp granite sand in equal proportions, The first 20 courses were further secured, in the same manner as the 1858 tower, by two $1\frac{1}{2}$ inch Muntz metal bolts, fox-wedged (a wedge for expanding the split end of a bolt to prevent it becoming loose), passing through the upper stone and nine inches into the stone below.

Once the dovetailed casing above mean tide level was complete, twelve workmen stayed at the tower so that they could work on the dressing back of the granite and other miscellaneous works when the weather allowed. This work was fairly

*Lifting stones from the* HERCULES *onto Bishop Rock lighthouse.*
FROM A BOOK OF THE SEA

dangerous but there were stringent safety measures in place. Each workman had a lifeline attached to a chain around the tower, and footboards were fixed to brackets secured in the masonry. A strong manila rope safety net beneath them gave the workforce a degree of confidence in their well-being on the rock. Domestically, their presence on the lighthouse must have affected the keepers' living and sleeping space!

For a change, Shearer & Co were managing to keep supplies of granite moving and, in February 1884, they sent a consignment destined for Bishop Rock to Wadebridge in Cornwall, presumably for shipment. But this efficiency was not to last and, by May, they were again late with supplies. However, they did manage to resume deliveries of granite and, by 29 October, 24 stones had been set in the 20th course while, by 19 November 1884, 457 stones comprising 22 courses had been set.

The lighthouse continued to progress; 24 June 1885 saw the workmen cutting stone for the 36th course, the 44th course was landed and set on 4 August, and the 51st course arrived and was set on 19 October.[4] Favourable weather extended the season in 1885 to 9 December, by which time 54 courses had been set.

*HERCULES attached to mooring buoys.*
FROM A BOOK OF THE SEA

As the works continued, gun metal fittings were required. Trinity House placed a notice in *The Times* on 2 October 1885 inviting tenders for 12 windows, eight shutters and sundry other fittings, all to be made from gun-metal and delivered to St Mary's. Harvey & Co's tender was accepted at £6 6s per hundredweight.

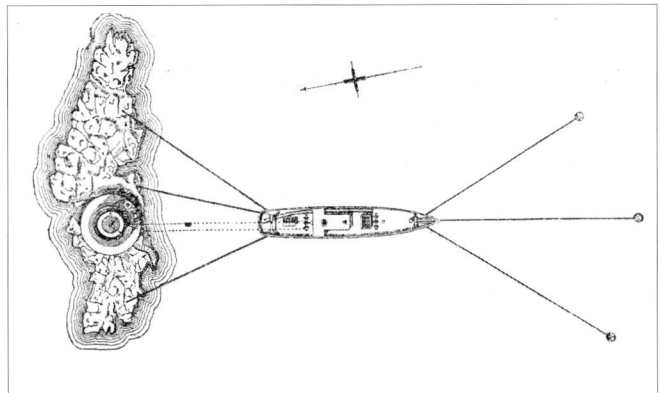

The granite blocks from the foundation level up to course sixty-two (set by 11 May 1886), had been lifted by a crane on the lantern gallery to their setting position where they were placed on the bed of cement. This was the limit of the dovetailed granite blocks. Demolition now began on the lantern and illuminating apparatus, which were removed for use elsewhere, together with the masonry forming the tower's service room. For this stage, a central crane was used. This consisted of a hollow wrought iron mast and top-mast, 40 feet in height, carried in iron partners and timbering in the rooms, and stayed by gun chains.

To dispose of the old masonry from the 1858 tower, a timber stage was constructed, together with rails and a truck. Into this truck a traversing jib lowered the stones, and it then ran along the rails to tip the stones clear of the tower and rock into the sea. Once the area had been cleared of the old stones, work began again on 26 June, building the rest of the tower comprising the four new rooms.

As each level of stone was completed, the crane was raised up by hydraulic jacks. To raise each new block of granite from its landing point on the rock, a steam boiler and winch were bolted to the vertical base of the platform, and a frame carrying two elm rollers enabled each stone to travel up the tower without any damage. This steam boiler and winch were later swept away during an equinoctial gale, but fortunately after the work had finished. In all, about one, or sometimes two courses, were laid per day, and the stonework (91 courses) was completed by 30 August 1886.

During the work to courses 63 to 91, when the lantern and illuminating apparatus had to be removed, a powerful double-flashing catoptric (where rays are directed from a light source into a concentrated beam by using a reflection from a mirror or parabolic reflector) light of a one-minute duration was temporarily installed in a Trinity House 'eight foot cylindrical floating light-lantern' hanging from an iron pole fixed to the top mast. The double flashing character of this temporary light was the same as that ordered for the new light. Its power was 16,000 candle power, whereas that of the old light had been 15,000. As with the crane, this had to be raised up by hydraulic jacks as work progressed. This light was exhibited from the lighthouse for the first time on 25 May 1886.

During this period of intense activity, other plans were being put into operation. Round Island, to the north of the Isles of Scilly, was purchased by Trinity House from Dorrien Smith in 1885 for the purpose of building another lighthouse and fog signal, the Board of Trade sanctioning the expenditure of £19,850 in October. But this was not the only plan afoot. One month later, Trinity House decided that the lighthouse on St Agnes should cease operating and a new light be built on Giants Castle Head, St Mary's. This work was to take place 1886-7, and the light was to be a first order dioptric (the largest available lens, 12 feet tall, six feet in diameter and a focal length of 36 inches), revolving every 30 seconds.

THE NEW LIGHT AND LANTERN

While construction work was in hand during 1885, a new light had been ordered for Bishop Rock lighthouse, comprising the highest power burner with a double flashing light every minute. An expenditure of £7,500 was allowed for these alterations and improvements and, of this,

*Plan of the 14ft lantern.*
TRINITY HOUSE

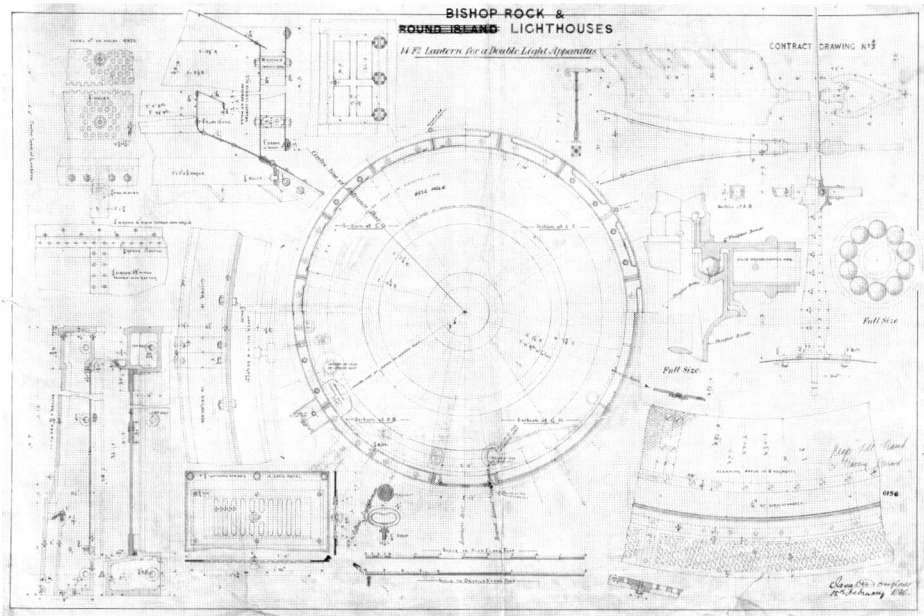

Chance Brothers
lantern under
construction.
M. BILLING SON
& CO, CHANCE
BROS ARCHIVE,
COURTESY
PETER WILLIAMS

£6,245 was allocated for the lantern and apparatus.

Tenders were invited for the lantern in March 1886, and that of Chance Bros & Co of Birmingham was accepted for both Bishop Rock and Round Island lighthouses. The new lantern comprised a cylindrical helical frame, 14 feet in diameter and the glazing 15 feet in height. The platform or murette was made from cast iron while the framing was of gun metal, and a thick copper sheet covered the steel 'rafters' or roof frame, supplied by the Thames Ironwork Company. The Old Delabole Slate Co provided the slate flooring, and T. & W. Ide supplied the plate-glass. The design of the roof allowed for ventilation of the interior without any down drafts, thus safeguarding the flame of the burners. The photograph (opposite) shows the ladder leading to the exterior catwalk. Taking into account the murette, glazing, roof and weathervane, the height of the lantern was 31 feet from top to bottom.[5]

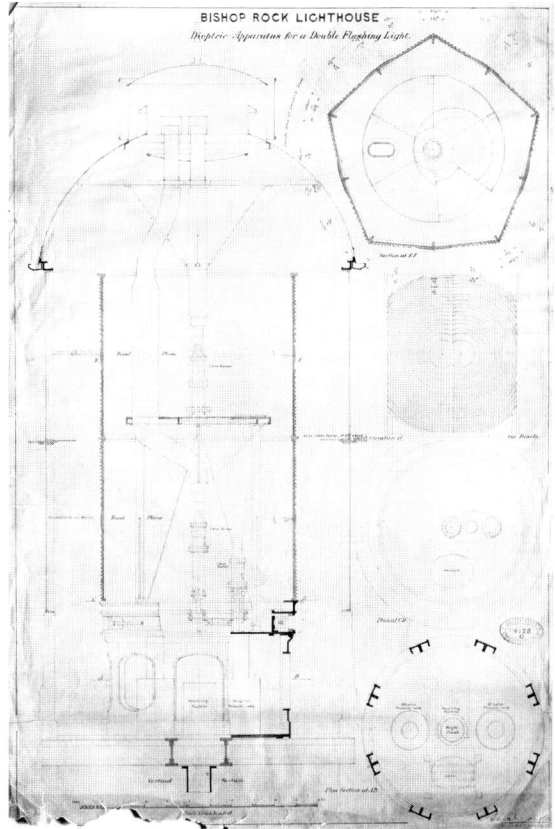

BISHOP ROCK LIGHTHOUSE
*Dioptric Apparatus for a Double Flashing Light.*

*Dioptric apparatus for double flashing light.*
TRINITY HOUSE

In August 1886, Chance Bros & Co also tendered to supply a biform dioptric apparatus for the new double flashing light at a cost of £3,321 14s. This was accepted, and they were instructed to make ones for Round Island and St Catherine's (Isle of Wight) lighthouses too.

When finished, the new optical apparatus, designed by W. F. A. Richey, had two superposed tiers of biform lenses with a focal distance of 1,330mm, known as hyper-radial, the greatest ever installed in a lighthouse. Each tier had ten panels, two panels to each set, each set containing two bull's eyes, and each bull's eye having 17 annular prisms, giving a double flash. The duration of flashes and eclipses are as follows:[6]

Flash 4³/₅ seconds
Eclipse 4³/₅ seconds
Flash 4³/₅ seconds
Eclipse 46¹/₅ seconds
Total period 60 seconds

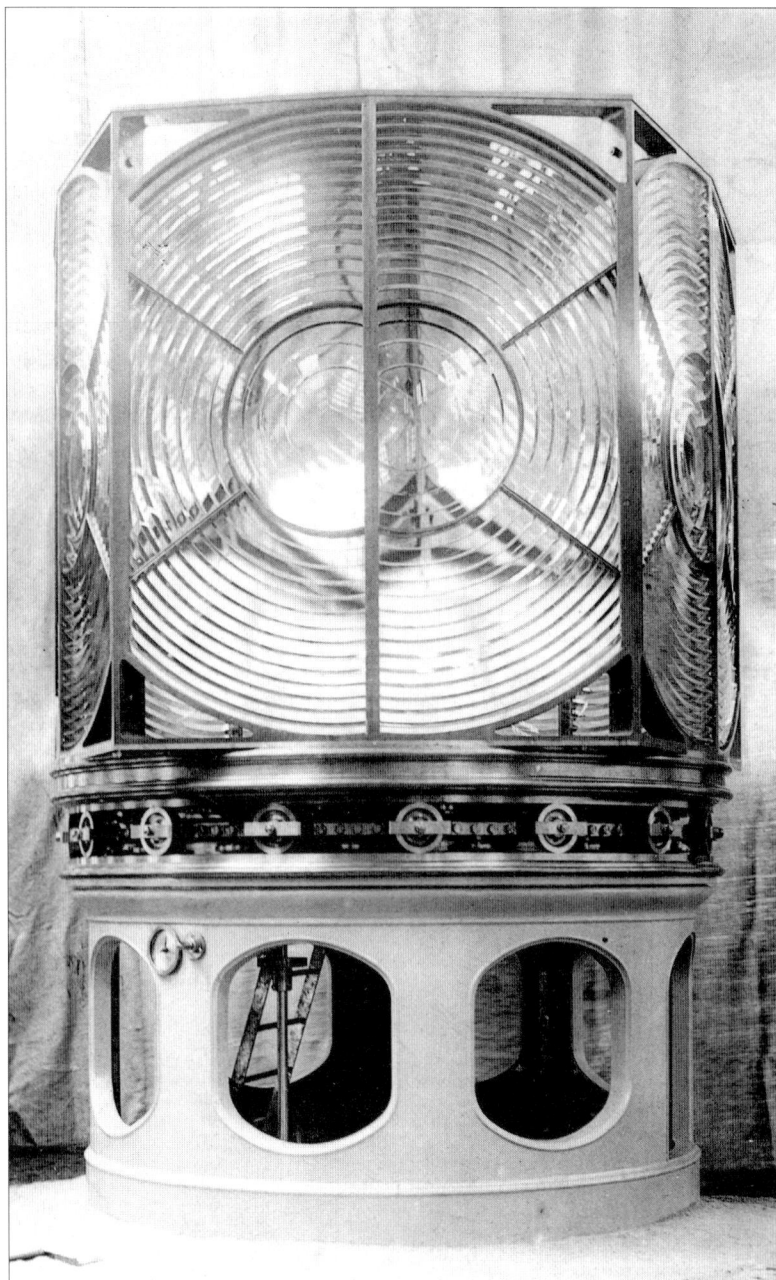

*The lower lens of the biform 1,330 mm focus lens at Bishop Rock.*
COURTESY PETER WILLIAMS AND ALK

*A typical Chance Bros biform lens complete.*
COURTESY PETER WILLIAMS AND ALK

When the weather was fine and visibility clear, the lower burner was transmitted at minimum power through the lower apparatus, giving a light of 40,000 candles to the horizon. When weather conditions were unfavourable and visibility reduced, the two burners were worked at maximum power. This gave a light through the double apparatus of

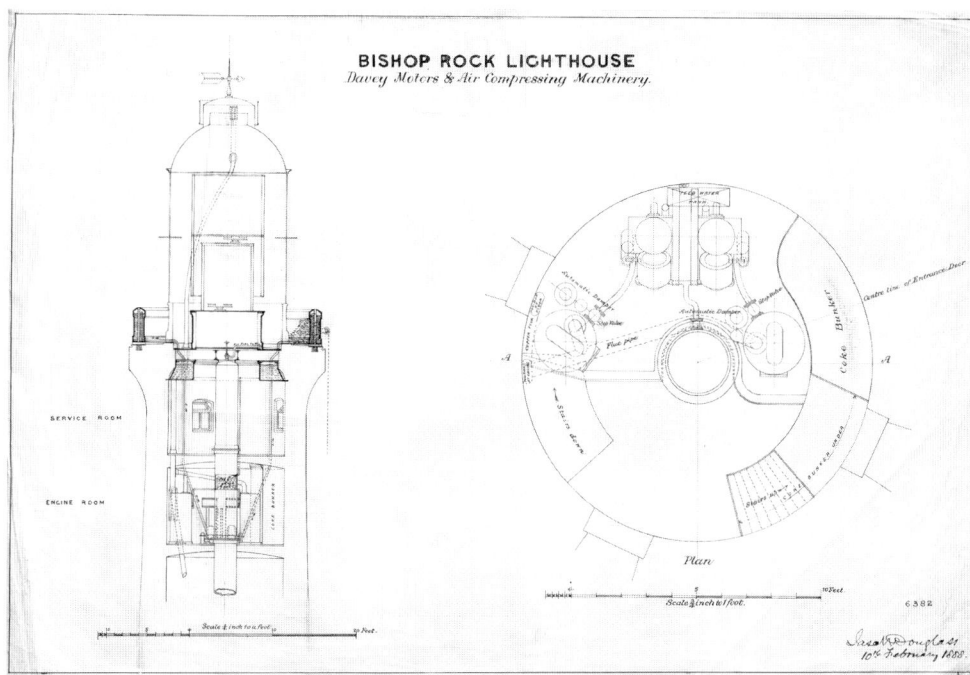

BISHOP ROCK LIGHTHOUSE
*Davey Motors & Air Compressing Machinery.*

230,000 candles. The criterion for changing from minimum to maximum was if St Agnes light could not be seen easily. To gain the most effectiveness from the flashes of the upper tier, these lenses focussed the flame from the burner onto the sea at a distance of five miles. The two 8-wick Trinity House burners, bought from Defries & Sons, were supplied with heavy mineral oil of 250 Fahrenheit flashing point.

The permanent light was finally exhibited for the first time on 25 October, 1887.

The power needed to rotate the illuminating apparatus's revolving machine could no longer be manual and needed special machinery to drive it. The Light Committee arranged with Douglass for a trial of a Davey motor engine at Blackwall in October 1887. This trial must have been successful because, in April 1888, the tender of Hathorn & Co for the supply of two 1¹/₂ effective h.p. Davey safety motors and air compressors at £420 was accepted. With these motors, sufficient air was compressed into two vertical air-receivers placed over-end at the centre of the tower. This worked a small air-engine in the pedestal of the illuminating apparatus, ensuring the latter kept rotating all night, and this machinery could be worked satisfactorily by the lighthouse keepers. The amount of coke needed for the Davey motors did not exceed 14 tons per year. The motors did not arrive together. After the first one had been in operation for a while, the other was delivered on 27 April 1889.[7]

*Plan of Davey Motors and Air Compressing Machinery.*
TRINITY HOUSE

*Crane for the gun
cotton firing
apparatus.*
TRINITY HOUSE

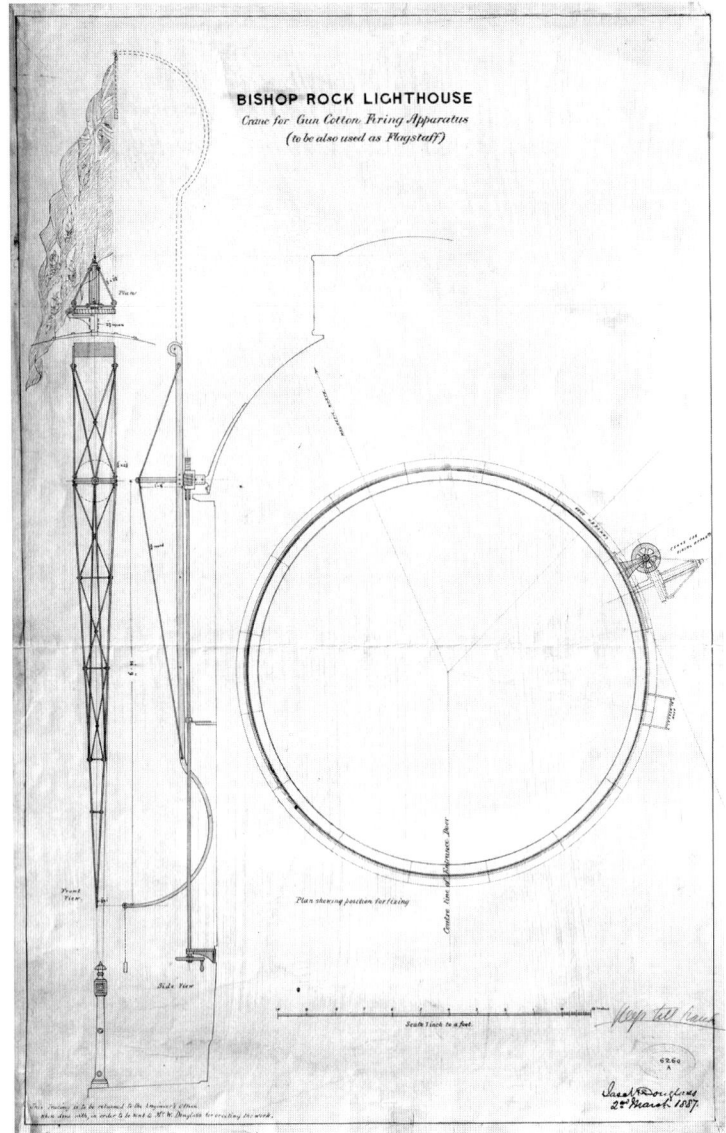

**BISHOP ROCK LIGHTHOUSE**
*Crane for Gun Cotton Firing Apparatus
(to be also used as Flagstaff)*

FOG SIGNAL

The question of fog signals raised itself again in November 1886. Trinity House hesitated to recommend the installation of a gun-cotton explosive fog signal (to replace the bell) at Bishop Rock if one was to be fitted at Round Island, as the sound would be too similar and might cause confusion. Finally, they did recommend one for Bishop Rock, with a distinctive character of a single discharge every 5 minutes. This was made on the assumption that an explosive signal would not be fitted on Round Island.

In January 1887 the estimated cost of £90 for the explosive fog signal was given, together with a further £209 2s p.a. needed for its maintenance, and was sanctioned by the Board of Trade. A notice appeared in *The Times* on 6 October 1887 advising mariners that an explosive fog signal had been established at Bishop Rock lighthouse which, during foggy weather, would give one report (sounding like the discharge of a gun) every five minutes.

The new gun cotton explosive fog signal, which was also used as a flagstaff, comprised a hollow steel jib attached to the lantern at roof level, and was worked by a worm wheel and pinion. To attach the gun-cotton charges, the jib was lowered and two charges suspended to the firing cables. These were connected with a dynamo electric 'exploder' (a plunger-operated electric firing apparatus) placed within the lantern. The jib was raised again and contact made at five minute intervals. Each charge comprised four ounces of gun-cotton into which a mercury detonator was placed before being suspended.

Discussing this in a paper given to the Institution of Civil Engineers in 1892, William Douglass said that during the years of encasing the original lighthouse, six wrecks took place in 'thick' weather within a radius of five miles of the tower. But since the introduction of the gun-cotton explosive fog signal (he claims in 1888), he was not aware of a single wreck within this radius in foggy weather.[8]

*Detail of the entrance door.*
TRINITY HOUSE

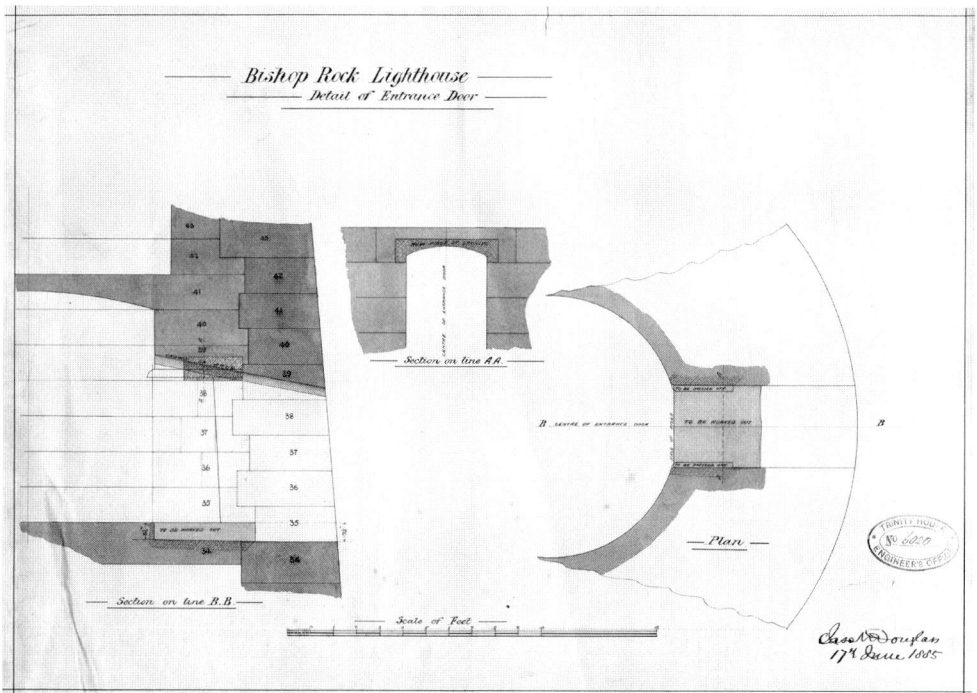

The five hundredweight fog bell that had been so ineffective was now discontinued, and the end of an era reached. This vital improvement for mariners had come twelve years too late for the victims of the *Schiller* disaster but, nevertheless, was to be welcomed as a major step forward in future seafaring safety.

At some stage, a mechanism for alerting lifeboats was installed at the lighthouse. 'Exploders' were obtained from a cotton powder company, and the signal was required to be substantially different from that of the fog signal, to avoid confusion for the lifeboatmen.

CONCLUSION OF THE WORKS

When the end of the building work was in sight, Douglass informed Trinity House that *Hercules* would not be required after December 1887, and that the lease on the workyard could be terminated. A small portion of the workyard was retained for Scilly lighthouses at a rent of £5 p.a. All spare material and plant on Bishop Rock lighthouse went to Penzance to be sold. According to local knowledge, some of the leftover stones were taken to the land on which Penold, a property in Old Town Road, St Mary's, was built. A resident made a gatepost for the garden from one of them.[9] Above the lighthouse door is the date 1887, together with the Trinity House Corporation's Arms, which are still there today.

The total weight of the tower was now, according to James Douglass, 6,000 tons. Only one block of stone had been lost from *Hercules* towards the end of the building work, caused by a heavy beam sea. This was quite remarkable given the nature of the swell that could suddenly rise up.

Of the conclusion to the works, William Douglass commented:

> It is very satisfactory to record that throughout the whole of the dangers incurred in the erection of the three lighthouses at this station, no loss of life or limb has ever occurred.
>
> The cost of the work executed at this station from time to time is as follows:[10]
>
> 1. Cast-iron lighthouse £12,500 0s 0d
> 2. Granite lighthouse £34,559 18s 9d
> 3. Improved granite lighthouse £64,889 0s 0d
> Total: £111,948 18s 9d
>
> If the usual test of cost for such structures is applied to the Bishop Rock lighthouse as it now stands, namely, per cubic foot of granite masonry, it amounts to £1 8s 6d, which compares favourably with other sea structures. On the other hand, if the value is estimated from a nautical point of view, at per unit of intensity of light provided, it will be found to be lower in cost than any other first-class sea lighthouse.

**BISHOP ROCK LIGHTHOUSE**

——— INSCRIPTION PLATE ———

¼ FULL SIZE

THIS TOWER WAS ERECTED BY
THE CORPORATION OF Trinity House OF DEPTFORD. STROND. LONDON.
THE FIRST STONE ONE OF THE 5TH COURSE WAS LAID ON THE 14TH JULY 1852 IN THE 16TH YEAR OF THE REIGN OF
Her Majesty Queen Victoria.
HIS GRACE THE Duke of Wellington MASTER
Captain Sir John Henry Pelly Bt. DEPUTY MASTER
THE LOWEST STONE WAS AFTERWARDS LAID IN A CHASM OF THE ROCK
AT ONE FOOT BELOW THE LEVEL OF LOW WATER SPRING TIDES ON THE 30TH JULY 1852
THE STONEWORK OF THE TOWER WAS FINISHED ON THE 28TH AUGUST 1857.
THE LIGHT WAS FIRST EXHIBITED ON THE 1ST SEPTEMBER 1858.
His Royal Highness The Prince Consort MASTER
Captain John Shepherd DEPUTY MASTER
THE SUCCESSFUL TERMINATION OF THIS MOST DIFFICULT UNDERTAKING WAS ACCOMPLISHED
WITHOUT LOSS OF LIFE OR SERIOUS ACCIDENT TO ANY PERSON EMPLOYED
"Deo Soli Gloria"

JAMES WALKER ENGINEER
NICHOLAS DOUGLASS SUPERINTENDENT

THE CYLINDRICAL BASE AT THE FOOT OF THIS TOWER, THE OUTER WALL,
AND THE THREE UPPER CHAMBERS, AND LANTERN WERE UNDERTAKEN BY
THE CORPORATION OF Trinity House IN ORDER TO OBTAIN INCREASED HEIGHT FOR THE LIGHT
AND GIVE GREATER STABILITY TO THE STRUCTURE.
THE FIRST STONE WAS LAID ON THE 21ST MAY 1883.
H.R.H. The Duke of Edinburgh K.G. MASTER.
Admiral Sir Richard Collinson K.C.B. DEPUTY MASTER.
THE STONEWORK WAS COMPLETED ON THE 3RD SEPTEMBER 1886
THE IMPROVED LIGHT WAS EXHIBITED AT FIRST TEMPORARILY ON THE 25TH MAY 1886
AND FROM THE HYPER-RADIAL OPTICAL APPARATUS ON THE 25TH OCTOBER 1887 IN THE REIGN OF
Her Majesty Queen Victoria
Admiral H.R.H. The Duke of Edinburgh MASTER.
Captain John Sydney Webb DEPUTY MASTER.
THIS ADDITIONAL UNDERTAKING WAS SCARCELY LESS DIFFICULT THAN THE FIRST
AND WAS MARKED BY A CONTINUANCE OF THE IMMUNITY FROM ACCIDENT COMMEMORATED ABOVE
"Unto Thee O Lord do we give thanks."

SIR JAMES NICHOLAS DOUGLASS F.R.S
ENGINEER-IN-CHIEF
WILLIAM TREGARTHEN DOUGLASS
RESIDENT ENGINEER

*Inscription Plate proposal.*
TRINITY HOUSE

Although, as William Douglass had pointed out, no lives were lost while working on the lighthouse it had been, nevertheless, dangerous and difficult work. One labourer, Matthew Andrews, commented that as work neared the lantern stage, 'the spray in a storm whipping up over the top was terrifying enough, but as the waves receded for the next onslaught, "it was like looking down into the jaws of hell" '.[11]

Trinity House had decided in December 1887 that, on completion of the tower, an inscription plate would be made to go inside. In early February 1888, Douglass submitted details for this, and it was given approval. Tenders were sought, and that of Forrest & Co's for £24 18s 6d was recommended and accepted. The inscription plate remains at the lighthouse today.

By August 1888 William Douglass had been appointed Inspector of Lights to the Indian Government. Therefore all extra works at Bishop Rock were to be finished by the end of the year, when his engagement would terminate.

Recalling his time at the lighthouse between 1981 and 1982, former PK Harold Taylor commented on these historic alterations:

> I found the lighthouse to be a peculiar sort of place because it had been built in two stages Strong metal ties showed where the extra thickness of stone had been bolted through the masonry. Higher up, from the kitchen level, the rest of the tower was reached by stone steps. This indicated where the alterations had been made.[12]

## SPECIFICATIONS OF THE 1887 LIGHTHOUSE

Height of Tower: 167ft

Height of Light above MHW: 142ft

Light Source: Pressure lamps supplying two 8-wick 'Trinity House Douglass' burners

Optic: Hyper Radial 1,330mm

Character: Double flashing light every minute

Candle Power: 40,000 normal / 230,000 in poor weather

Range of Light: 18 1/4 miles

Fog Warning Apparatus: Gun-cotton explosive, giving one report every five minutes

Cost: £64,889

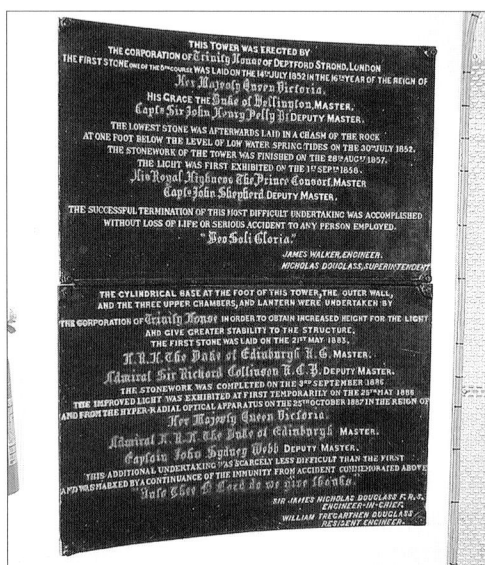

*Inscription Plate.*
TRINITY HOUSE

# CHAPTER SEVEN

# 1889 TO 1899

## MINOR REPAIRS AND ALTERATIONS

The life of Bishop Rock lighthouse continued relatively uneventfully over the next few years with no major incidents. Repairs were constantly needed, such as repointing the tower, and new parts were often required as sea, weather, wear and tear all took their toll.

The upper light became problematic as it was occasionally extinguished by the fog signal explosives. William Douglass, who was still on hand for advice, recommended that when the fog signal was in operation, two burners should be lighted on the outer wicks only. More problems arose when, in May 1893, two panels of the dioptric apparatus became loose through firing of the fog signal. Douglass proposed that all panels should be strengthened at a cost of £80, and that a gun metal stay should be placed across the panels of the apparatus.

A Distress Signal was introduced in 1893:

By day    2 explosive rockets every 5 minutes.
By night  2 explosive rockets every 5 minutes followed by a Light Service
          Rocket (a visual signal) ten seconds after each double report.

In February 1893 Trinity House expressed an interest in seeing if the lighting apparatus could be rotated by clockwork, and the matter was further investigated in 1897. In July the engineer advised that in the following year's estimates they should allow for the existing Davey motors to be replaced with revolving machinery. But it was not until the early 1900s that the changeover was put in hand. In the meantime, repairs to the Davey motors and optical apparatus would cost £160.

Other items also needed attention. A flashing signal lamp was purchased in 1897, a new ventilation waste pipe was installed at £20, a boiler was damaged and the cost of repair was £90, to include an overhaul of the machinery. But boilers continued to cause problems. The construction of a special boiler for the Davey motor was needed, plus a new copper flue costing £70.

The oil tank was fitted with glass gauges at a cost of £5, and £45 had to be spent rectifying a defect in the fog signal engine as it was impossible to maintain a proper vacuum. This was affecting the cleaning of the condensers.

## THE KEEPERS

Keepers came and went much as usual during this time. They had had to live with years of building work going on around them which could not have been easy, especially for those on night watch who needed to sleep by day. The noise must have been excessive at times, and space somewhat cramped with the daily accommodation of workmen and their supplies.

Sadly, one keeper, Samuel Rambridge died in office on 24 July 1894; he was only 49 years old and left a wife, Selina. He is buried in Old Town Church, St Mary's. Selina may have returned to the mainland as her name does not appear on the gravestone.

*The grave of keeper Samuel Rambridge.*
ELISABETH
STANBROOK

The keepers' lives were not without incident and, it has to be said, some of these were self-inflicted. On 1 January 1889 it transpired that the Bishop Rock light had been lit late on 29 November. This was a major offence and, consequently, Trinity House recommended that AK M. Pender, 'be severely reprimanded for his serious neglect of duty, and that his good conduct money be withheld until further orders, the Supt to report periodically as to his behaviour'.[1]

But this was not all. Damage had occurred through a 'wrong firing' of the explosive fog signal. Two Assistant Keepers, Mitchell and Dunsford were also 'reprimanded for their carelessness'.

AK Fenn found himself in trouble in July 1893. He somehow caused the 8-wick burner to catch fire, and was consequently required to pay £5 towards the repair of the lamp in monthly instalments of 10s.

Two years later, AK Boulton was 'reprimanded for his carelessness' in firing the fog signal which resulted in damage. He was required to pay £10 in monthly instalments of £1 towards the costs of repair. Later he suffered a bout of ill health and was initially granted £2 towards his expenses from the Medical Donation Fund. But his £10 fine caught up with him, and this was reduced to £8 instead.

In early February 1896, the Principal Keeper, W. Jones, received a caution and severe reprimand for failing to return to duty after a trip to London.

Subtle changes to their employment took place. On 12 November 1889 a SAK arrived on the lighthouse for duty during the winter months and, a year later in November 1890, a Supernumerary Keeper was allowed on a permanent basis. Towards the end of March 1891 the appointment of another keeper was sanctioned. The order was also given that all vacancies at Round Island were to be filled from Bishop Rock as they occurred, from July 1892. By 1897 Trinity House was stipulating that no keeper should stay at Bishop Rock for more than two years.

On a more domestic level, in 1897 the keepers were provided with a supply of bed curtains, £20 was spent on raising the skirting boards in the men's bed berths by 1 foot, the sleeping bunks were lined, a new oak locker was fitted for storage of the keepers' food at a cost of £10, and improvements to the sanitary arrangements and water supply were undertaken for £60.

The keepers' dwellings on St Mary's saw the overhauling of the drainage and water supply at a cost of £100, which was superintended by Mr J. Seldon, while the roofs were repaired by Mr H. Nelson for £10 18s.

With the building of Round Island lighthouse in 1887, the Trinity House dwellings were re-allocated: two for Bishop Rock and two for Round Island. Other Bishop Rock keepers found their own accommodation elsewhere on St Mary's.

A circular was printed in March 1899 which gave the daily rates of pay for lighthouse keepers:

Supernumerary Keepers: Unqualified 2s 6d
Supernumerary Keepers: Qualified 3s 0d
Assistant Keepers, on appointment 3s 0d
    after 5 years service 3s 2d
    after 10 years service 3s 4d
    after 15 years service 3s 6d
Principal Keepers, on appointment 3s 9d
    after 5 years service 3s 11d
    after 10 years service 4s 2d

## TRAGEDY AT BISHOP ROCK

It was towards the end of 1898 that a tragedy unfolded at Bishop Rock when, on 19 December, the distress signal was given from the lighthouse at 8pm. No relief was required until the following morning, presumably indicated via the flashing signal lamp installed the year before, fuelling speculation that a death had taken place. On arrival at the lighthouse, it was discovered that PK John Ball was missing, presumed drowned. At

*Principal Keeper*
*John Ball.*
STAN AND
MARGRET
BUTCHER
(LIGHTHOUSE
DUO)

about 3.30pm he had gone outside onto the rock for some air and to smoke his pipe. He did not re-appear to exhibit the light or complete his watch, and he could not be found by his colleagues. The sea had been calm, so it was supposed that he felt giddy or lost his balance and fell into the sea. His body was never found, and Trinity House gave his widow, Mrs Theresa Ball a pension. He left eight children.

The London Assurance Corporation (LAC) wrote to Trinity House in January 1899 enquiring about the disappearance of John Ball, and requesting affidavits from the other keepers, which were subsequently obtained.

In February, LAC accepted the evidence provided about the death of John Ball, and agreed to pay out £166 in due course. John Ball's children had also been interviewed and stated that they 'have nothing to urge against the proceeds of the insurance being paid to the mother'.

Having no reason to remain on the Isles of Scilly, Mrs Ball decided to return to the mainland. In April, the Superintendent of Penzance sent Trinity House a letter from her asking for expenses for moving to Sennen. This was approved, and so ended a very sad chapter in the life of one keeper and his family. It was also a sad note on which to end the nineteenth century.

THE RELIEF

In mid-November 1887, the Light Committee had recommended that Obadiah Hicks should continue to provide relief for Bishop Rock lighthouse in his gig *O & M*. Later that month, his terms of business were accepted, which also included Round Island:

Monthly relief each £2 10s
Extra trips £2 10s
Unsuccessful trips £1 5s
Keeping station supplied with coals and water £4 10s per three months (increased to £5 in July 1899).
Ditto with oil £1 3s per drum

The nature of the reliefs also changed. In 1891, a payment of £48 p.a. was made for fortnightly reliefs instead of the £30 p.a. paid for monthly reliefs. This meant that each keeper would be at the station only one month instead of two, and have two weeks shore leave. The boat hire arrangements with Obadiah Hicks were modified, with an increase of £1 per quarter for landing the coal and water.

In 1896 Hicks retired as relief boatman and asked Trinity House for a pension. But they refused as his working life had not been devoted entirely to them. So, in December, he applied for a gratuity to which they eventually agreed, awarding him £30. Trinity House did pay tribute to his relief work, recognising that he had performed an arduous and dangerous service without accident for a long continuous period.

In July 1896, the Light Committee recommended the appointment of William Hicks of St Agnes as relief boatman for both Bishop Rock and Round Island, on the same terms as Obadiah, until the arrival of a new steam vessel (which was, in fact, never used for this purpose). Relief trips were paid at £2 10s.

It would seem that a visit to the interior of Bishop Rock lighthouse was a tourist attraction at the turn of the nineteenth century. The

*Homeland Handbook* for the Isles of Scilly gives a fascinating insight into life on the lighthouse at this time:

> The lower door, which is on the south-east side, is gained by means of a brass ladder. The door is of brass, and from it a spiral staircase leads up to the lower room, in which is kept water, coal and other stores. Above the store-room is the kitchen, which is followed by the bedroom, and the service-room, respectively. In the latter is a library and above it is the lantern. A reserve store of provisions is kept in the lighthouse by the Trinity Board. Three men are always in residence while the fourth is on leave. The relief is timed for every four weeks, but owing to heavy weather it is not an uncommon occurrence for it to be two, three, and even six weeks over time. The oil and other stores are landed annually from one of the Trinity yachts, on the occasion of the visit of the Elder Brethren.
>
> The men who serve the Bishop have a trying and nerve-destroying time and look thoroughly done up after their spell is over. Visitors are courteously welcomed by them, and if, from the plenitude of our books and newspapers, we could only remember to send an occasional post packet to the lonely watchers on the Bishop it would be very gratefully received.

Plans for Giants Castle Head lighthouse had continued apace throughout these years. Although put on hold in April 1887, by November the decision was made to spend £15,000 on building it, and then discontinue the light on St Agnes. Bishop Rock tolls were to be

*Giants Castle Head.*
ELISABETH STANBROOK

*The lighthouse inset in the rock From A Book of the Sea*

doubled to help defray the costs. Finally, the new lighthouse for Giants Castle Head was given the go-ahead in July 1899.

And so the nineteenth century closed, having seen one of England's most important lighthouses built in the south west, constructed on a rock in a notorious stretch of water, thus saving many a ship and her crew from disaster. The twentieth century was to see huge changes in the lighthouse service on all levels, from general maintenance to new technology, and from keepers to automation.

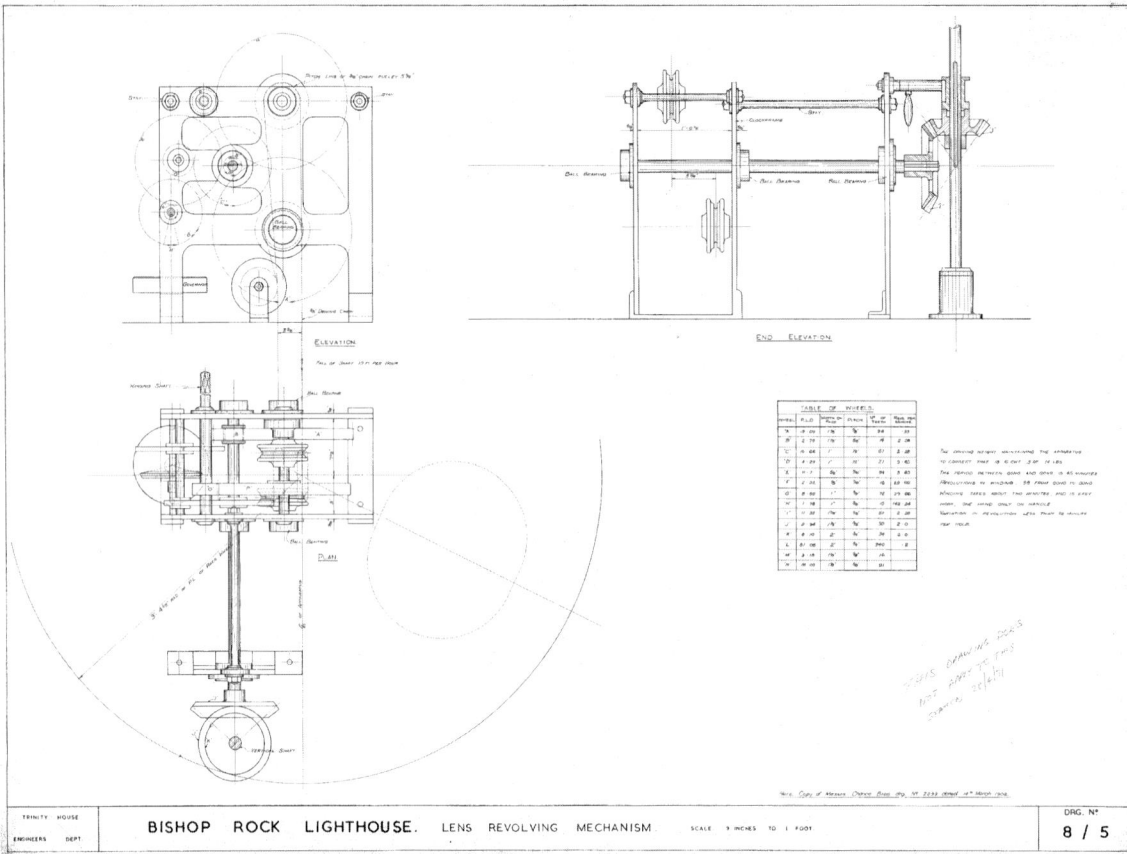

*Lens revolving mechanism.* TRINITY HOUSE

# CHAPTER EIGHT

# 1900 TO 1913

The pre-Great War period for Bishop Rock lighthouse and its occupants had its ups and downs, and repairs and alterations continued apace. Outside bodies were starting to find it a useful venue for various studies. For example, in April 1901, Lloyds made an enquiry by 'electrical communication' (an early use of wireless) as to whether Trinity House would allow a man to perform signalling at Bishop Rock, from where he would transmit messages by 'aetheric' signalling apparatus to Scilly. Trinity House approved this, but refused permission for an additional man to be stationed at the lighthouse to make signals to passing vessels.

Three years later, in April 1904, the Geological Survey & Museum, Jermyn Street, London requested assistance in obtaining geological specimens from Bishop Rock, Eddystone, Longships and Wolf Rock lighthouses in connection with a re-survey of Cornwall that was now in progress. Trinity House was happy to assist and instructed the engineer to obtain specimens as opportunities occurred.

THE LIGHT – MAJOR CHANGES

Changes were made to the light during this time. At the end of February 1902 the engineer sent Trinity House an estimate of £896 for replacing the Davey motor and air receivers with new revolving machinery. The following month, they also received a tender of £170, from Chance Brothers & Co, for the clock required in connection with this. The Light Committee thought it prudent to recommend an additional sum of £130 to be added to the estimate. Mr Seccombe, a Trinity House mechanic from Blackwall, plus three workmen, were landed on Bishop Rock on 8 July. They removed the Davey motors and the boilers, and prepared for the arrival of the new gear for the revolving clockwork machinery, which was landed on 25 September.[1]

The installation of this machinery was a success, despite another £98 required for it shortly afterwards. The clock which drove it sat underneath the lens and, when fully wound, would drive the machinery for one hour and ten minutes, after which, it needed rewinding. A governor was attached to the clock, responsible for the true colour of the light, and had two springs with corks at the ends to regulate the clock's speed.[2]

During 1903 plans for a new oil burner were approved. Thus, a new triple-mantle Matthews incandescent oil burner light was, on the night of 23 August 1904, satisfactorily exhibited, which the Superintendent of the Light Committee considered a great improvement. A few months later, it was decided that the light should be burnt on full power in all weathers. It may be these alterations to the light that increased its intensity to 720,000 candle power and a range of 25 nautical miles.

Chance Bros & Co were asked to provide various other pieces of equipment during 1909 and 1910, including an acetylene lamp costing £15, a new mercury float and pedestal at £703 6s, and a wrought iron trimming stage required in connection with the improvement of the light for £65.

Only four years after the new incandescent oil burner was installed, Trinity House decided upon alterations to the character of the light. The Board of Trade sanctioned the expenditure of £1,600 for this purpose, with £600 to be spent during 1912-3, but by July the cost of this had risen to £1,709. The character of the proposed light was a white group flashing (2) every 15 seconds:

| | |
|---|---|
| Flash | 1 second |
| Eclipse | $1^{1}/_{4}$ seconds |
| Flash | 1 second |
| Eclipse | $11^{3}/_{4}$ seconds |
| Total | 15 seconds |

These alterations were carried out by Mr Riley, another Trinity House mechanic from Blackwall. The higher and lower lenses were stored in the Engine and Service Rooms. In mid-December 1912, work having been in progress for some time, the engineer announced that the exhibition of the new light could take place on the night of 19 June 1913. The order was given that a notice be issued to mariners, but that it was to omit the information that there would be a decrease in intensity of light for two months prior to the alteration!

Work on the new light continued meanwhile, but a hitch nearly postponed the exhibition of the light. The engineer found defects in the castings of the light's new pedestal, and he asked for a postponement. Fortunately, the problem was overcome and the exhibition took place with temporary apparatus on the evening of 19 June, according to the original plan. This character of light is the one currently exhibited at Bishop Rock.

The following month, Keller Bryant & Co, London, suggested that the Bishop Rock light be exhibited by day during fog, as was being undertaken experimentally at the Eddystone lighthouse. The reply was not recorded.

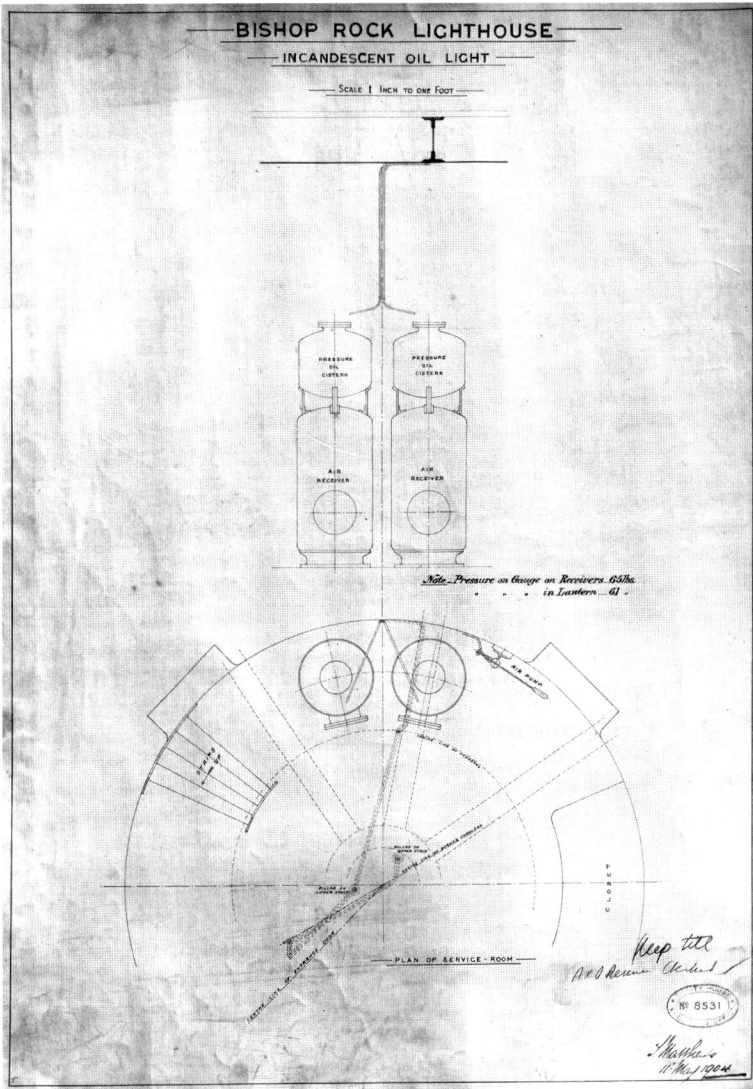

*The incandescent oil burner 1904.* TRINITY HOUSE

GENERAL MAINTENANCE

General maintenance during this time included the repairing of old boilers, repointing the tower, and interior painting undertaken by Mr J. P. Oates. He was paid £2 per week.

The firm Ellis & Sons was paid £2 15s for whitewashing St Mary's cottages. The dwellings needed regular attention, and Ellis & Sons also repaired the drainage system for £52 10s, and later cleaned the drains and provided siphons at a cost of £3 17s 6d. Repairs to the roof and gutters were also undertaken, and the firm Colenso & Co were paid £40 for painting the dwellings. Two of the gardens were found to be badly kept in 1905 after an inspection, especially that of AK Thompson. He was ordered to keep the weeds down. But six years later, the gardens still looked in a neglected state with an abundance of weeds. It was suggested that the gardens were too big for the keepers to manage.

In 1910 the Board of Trade sanctioned the spending of £300 for a submarine bell and buoy, fitted with an aerial bell, off Bishop Rock, to be made by Messrs Pintack. This signalling apparatus was a type of underwater fog bell. Thick fog does, of course, obscure the light emanating from a lighthouse. Fog signals are then brought into use, but these have varying degrees of audibility due to the variations in density of the fog and air. Water, however, is an excellent conductor of sound as it travels much faster and without hindrance. Ships with receiving apparatus pick up the signal without having to rely on an air-borne one.

The next year, the Submarine Signal Company was paid £240 to supply two sets of submarine bell buoy mechanisms required for both Bishop Rock and Eddystone, and the former was installed on 18 March 1911. In August, the engineer suggested that receiving apparatus be fitted to enable the keepers to listen to the sounding of the submarine bell buoy.

By January 1912 the Bishop Rock buoy was reported to be out of action, and it was taken to Penzance in June. Trinity House were annoyed at this delay, feeling that if it had been brought in sooner, the damage would have been a lot less. The inner tube or pipe had broken off close to the cogs, one corner of the cog chamber was gone, and the float and broken inner tube had completely disappeared. All the hammers on the aerial bell had disappeared and the platform from which they had hung was completely adrift, but were subsequently secured upside down on the bell. The wooden battens were much worn and chafed, although intact, the wooden fender being in the same condition but with some sections gone.

## KEEPERS

Changes to the period of duty at Bishop Rock lighthouse were made in 1901. In April, Trinity House had given permission for an Assistant Keeper to stay on Bishop Rock for another two years, despite the ruling of 1897. In November, they decided the ruling that no keeper was to be kept there for longer than two years, and that all vacancies at Round Island being filled from Bishop Rock, be rescinded, and suggested these rulings had been irregular.

With the installation of the new clockwork machinery in 1903, the engineer was of the opinion that one keeper might be permanently withdrawn from the station. After consideration, Trinity House reduced the lighthouse staff (which had been one Principal Keeper and five

Assistant Keepers) by two Assistant Keepers, and decided that a Supernumerary Keeper was, once more, to be sent to do duty at the station during the winter months as at other rock stations in the district. However, the decision about the SAK post was rescinded in November 1904, after the new incandescent oil burner came into use.

Trinity House found themselves having to deal with another act of misconduct by keepers in July 1903. AK McBride and SK W. H. Pollard (from another lighthouse) had submitted false accounts of travelling expenses supported by forged vouchers. They each claimed 21s for the hire of the same trap (for which the proper total charge was 24s). This resulted in their dismissal from the service and a demand for a refund of the amount they overcharged. Also, Principal Keepers were, in future, to countersign vouchers for 'trap-hire'.

Another tragedy struck on 13 August 1903 with the accidental drowning of AK Sidney Hicks. As the relief boat was approaching Bishop Rock with stores, Hicks went down onto the rock to fasten the mooring rope to an eye bolt embedded in it. On his way back, he slipped off the set-off and fell down onto the rocks below, and a rising wave washed him away. Although his cap was retrieved by the relief crew, he was never seen again. His father, crewman Osbert Hicks, underwent the trauma of witnessing this event.

Hicks was replaced by SAK J. B. Paskell. Losing his son while on duty did not deter Osbert Hicks from informing Trinity House that he would like another son, Fred, aged 22, to become a lighthouse keeper. He was currently at Penzance working as a blacksmith.

Recalling his experiences of duty on a tower lighthouse in the 1970s, a keeper explained how easy it was to be swept off the set-off by waves. On one occasion he had been helping to land supplies from the boat below, in calm seas, when suddenly an enormous wave appeared and, had he not been hooked on to a safety harness, he would have been washed out to sea.

The estimates for work in 1908-9 included building the new lighthouse on Giants Head Castle in lieu of that on St Agnes. But, in the end, Trinity House decided against this and chose Peninnis Head on which to site one instead, at an estimated cost of £2,600. This new lighthouse, which started operating in 1911, had no attached accommodation for keepers so, in September, it was decided that keepers from Bishop Rock and Round Island, when ashore, would be paid 10s a month for attending to it. This practice continued until Mr W. J. Coleman was made its Principal Keeper in April 1947.

It would seem that up to 1913, keepers had kept their provisions in drawers under their beds. But lockers were recommended to be built for this purpose in the now empty former engine room.

THE RELIEFS

On display in the Isles of Scilly Museum is the gig *Klondyke*, said to have been bought for £8 in 1897, for the Bishop Rock lighthouse reliefs and pilot work. No supporting evidence has been found for this claim but, if correct, the gig must have been used during William Hicks's relief contract.

The reliefs continued to be exercised by William Hicks for a few years. In 1901 he applied for an advance to enable him to obtain a new relief boat. He suggested the Corporation paid two-thirds of the cost. No decision was recorded.

After a request from the keepers that the reliefs become monthly so that they could have a month ashore instead of two weeks (but two months on the lighthouse), Trinity House voted in October 1905 by 5-3 that the Bishop Rock reliefs be monthly again in future. They made enquiries of the Light Committee as to what modifications could be made accordingly in the current boat hire. However, none seemed possible as William Hicks was insisting upon £60 p.a. for effecting the reliefs if they changed. Trinity House was not happy with this and asked if there was anyone else who could undertake them. But to no avail, so he was informed that, unless he reduced his charge, the Elder Brethren would consider other arrangements for reliefs at Round Island.

By December, having got nowhere, the Light Committee recommended that three months' notice be given to William Hicks to terminate the present agreement of boat hire, and that a new agreement be put in force at the expiration of the notice. So, in January 1906, the Board of Trade sanctioned payment of £3 for each monthly relief of Bishop Rock in lieu of £2 10s for the present fortnightly relief. This arrangement continued for just over a year, until William Hicks's contract was actually terminated. Trinity House decided his final pay should be £3 instead of £12 as he had not carried out his contract satisfactorily.

A replacement contract was drawn up in January 1907 for effecting the reliefs at Bishop Rock and Round Island lighthouses for three years with Mr Israel Hicks and his boat *Elaine*. This was on the same terms as William Hicks, except during the work being done to install the new light in 1913, when he received an extra £3 per quarter for taking fresh water out to the lighthouse. It has been claimed that Israel undercut his cousin William to get the contract,[3] but as payment was the same as the final year, it may have been that he was more willing to accept Trinity House's terms. Local memory also recalls that one of the relief boats Israel used during his time as contractor was the *Belle of the Bay*, which had a motor.[4]

On 23 September 1909 relief crew member William George Mortimer's hand was severely injured when at Bishop Rock. He applied for compensation, but Trinity House's solicitor said his claim should be against Israel Hicks the contractor. It was not recorded whether Mr Mortimer ever made such a claim.

### SHIPPING DISASTERS NEAR BISHOP ROCK

This pre-War period saw various wrecks in the vicinity of the lighthouse. On 22 June 1901, the Liverpool barque *Falkland* hit the west side of Bishop Rock in fog at 7.20pm, her main yard striking the lighthouse itself. A jagged part of the rock below the surface of the sea rent her hull, and she sank within about ten minutes.

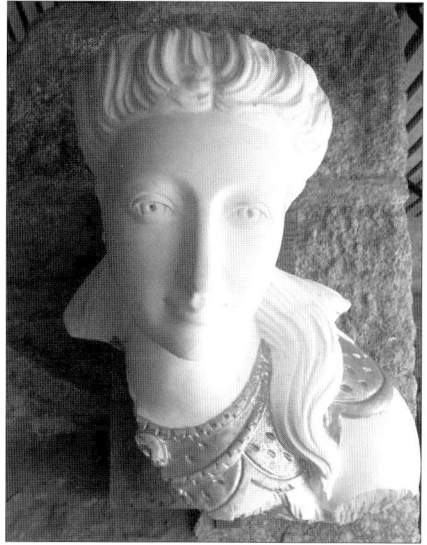

*Damaged head from the ship* FALKLAND *at Valhalla Museum, Tresco.*
ELISABETH STANBROOK

On 19 June 1909 at 3pm, the ship *Leon Bureau* struck rocks near the lighthouse, again during fog, despite the sounding of the fog signal. On the night of 17 April 1910, the Atlantic Transport Line Steamer *Minnehaha* became stranded on the outer rocks of Scilly, again despite the sounding of Bishop Rock's fog signal.

But it was the wreck of another vessel that caused the most consternation. Unluckily, it was on Friday 13 December 1907 that a huge seven-masted steel schooner, the *Thomas W. Lawson* from Boston foundered off the Western Rocks at Minmanueth, near Annet during a terrific storm. She was carrying a cargo of 2,225,000 gallons of light oil from Pennsylvania to London. In fog and snow, and mistaking Bishop Rock lighthouse for a passing ship, she had sailed inside the Crim Rocks. Realising the mistake, two anchors were dropped in the hope that she would be safe until the storm passed. Alarmed at what they saw, the lighthouse keepers fired distress signals at around 4pm which alerted both St Agnes and St Mary's lifeboat crews.

*THOMAS W LAWSON belt at Valhalla Museum, Tresco.*
ELISABETH STANBROOK

The St Agnes crew were first on the scene, comprising coxswain William George Mortimer, William Thomas (Cook) Hicks, his son Frederick Charles (Cook) Hicks, second coxswain Abraham James Hicks, his son James Thomas Hicks, Obadiah Hicks, William Francis Hicks, Albert Hicks, Stephen Lewis Hicks, Jack Hicks, Fred Hicks, William Treneary, Ben Hicks and Walter Long (names vary according to whose account you read). On reaching the stricken vessel, its Captain, George Dow, asked for a pilot, and so William Thomas Hicks boarded her.

The St Mary's lifeboat, *Henry Dundas*, which had

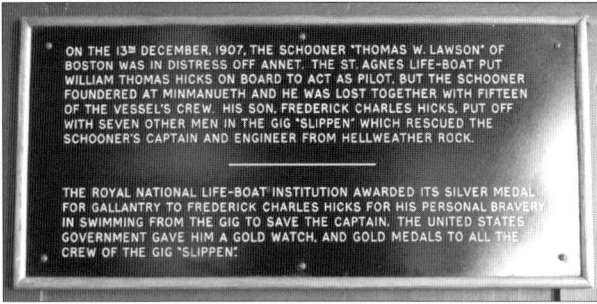

ON THE 13ᵀᴴ DECEMBER, 1907, THE SCHOONER "THOMAS W. LAWSON" OF BOSTON WAS IN DISTRESS OFF ANNET. THE ST. AGNES LIFE-BOAT PUT WILLIAM THOMAS HICKS ON BOARD TO ACT AS PILOT, BUT THE SCHOONER FOUNDERED AT MINMANUETH AND HE WAS LOST TOGETHER WITH FIFTEEN OF THE VESSEL'S CREW. HIS SON, FREDERICK CHARLES HICKS, PUT OFF WITH SEVEN OTHER MEN IN THE GIG "SLIPPEN" WHICH RESCUED THE SCHOONER'S CAPTAIN AND ENGINEER FROM HELLWEATHER ROCK.

THE ROYAL NATIONAL LIFE-BOAT INSTITUTION AWARDED ITS SILVER MEDAL FOR GALLANTRY TO FREDERICK CHARLES HICKS FOR HIS PERSONAL BRAVERY IN SWIMMING FROM THE GIG TO SAVE THE CAPTAIN. THE UNITED STATES GOVERNMENT GAVE HIM A GOLD WATCH, AND GOLD MEDALS TO ALL THE CREW OF THE GIG "SLIPPEN".

*Plaque in St Agnes Church.*
ELISABETH STANBROOK

arrived in the meantime, was compelled to return to harbour after becoming damaged and, later, the St Agnes lifeboat *Charles Deere James*, had to do the same when crew member William Francis Hicks became ill. Bad weather prevented her return to the *Thomas W. Lawson*, but a watch was kept for distress signals. None sounded and the Bishop Rock lighthouse keepers reported that they last saw the schooner's lights moving eastwards at about 2.10 or 2.20am. As she had not arrived in St Mary's by daybreak, it became obvious that all was not well, especially when quantities of light oil appeared on the beaches. Tragedy had struck with the sinking of the schooner near Shag Rock, and the loss of fifteen crew members plus William Hicks, the pilot who had stayed on board. The two surviving men, the Captain and the engineer, were found on Hellweathers and were saved by the pilot's son, Frederick Hicks. He had set out from St Agnes with other crewmen (Israel Hicks, Obadiah Hicks, Osbert Hicks and his son Jack, Grenfell Legg, William Treneary and William George Mortimer) in the gig *Slippen* to rescue them.

A plaque in St Agnes Church records:

> The Royal National Life-boat Institution awarded its silver medal for gallantry to Frederick Charles Hicks for his personal bravery in swimming from the gig to save the Captain. The United States Government gave him a gold watch, and gold medals to all the crew of the gig "Slippen".

Later that month, Trinity House received a rather sad letter from Mrs Elizabeth A. Hicks of St Agnes, widow of the drowned pilot William Hicks, applying for financial assistance as her husband had been the former relief boatman. He had left behind a family of young children. In January 1908, they granted her the sum of fifty guineas (£52 10s.).

On 8 January 1911, the sailing ship *Ardencraig* foundered in thick fog having struck the Gunners. She had been en route from Melbourne to Cardiff and laden with grain. In response to distress guns fired from Bishop Rock lighthouse, the lifeboats from St Agnes and St Mary's were launched together with the lighthouse relief boat. All crew were saved. The Court of Inquiry expressed its high appreciation of alertness and decision of the Bishop Rock keepers, and recommended that they should be commended for their prompt action.

# Chapter Nine

# The Great War years

Trinity House records do not reveal much about how these years impinged upon life in the tower. We do know that various steamers and ships were torpedoed by German submarines off Scilly; for example, on 3 February 1917 *Housatonic* was went down off Bishop Rock after an attack by *U-53*, while on 23 February, seven Dutch and one Norwegian ships were attacked west of Bishop Rock. Three of these ships sank, and the St Agnes lifeboat and other vessels from that and other islands put to sea to help the survivors and escort the damaged ships to St Mary's, for which they received medals from the Netherlands section of the League of Neutral Nations.[1]

An RAF pilot's aircraft had engine failure and plunged into the sea off Bishop Rock in June 1918.

Some lighthouse keepers departed temporarily to take part in war duties. For example, in November 1916, AK Blair left for military duty, his place taken by a temporary AK, while on 14 October 1917, AK L. H. Mitchell was granted a Commission while he was on active service.

Before AK Blair left for duty, he had an accident on 16 June 1916 when he fell the 40 feet from the set-off to the rocks below. He was severely bruised but able to perform light duties within about ten days. As a result, Trinity House took unspecified precautions to ensure the safety of the keepers while working on the landings.

The rates for relief boat hire increased from 1 April 1917 for the duration of the war. Whether this was back-paid to 1914 is not recorded:

Bishop Rock monthly relief - £3 10s.
Supplying coal and water to Bishop Rock - £7 per quarter
Round Island monthly relief - £2 5s.

Israel Hicks had a motor fitted in his boat, now the *Arizona*, in 1914. As a consequence, he requested permission either to use one man less in his crew, or increased remuneration. Initially both were refused, but later in May Trinity House granted permission for him to have a crew of four rather than five.

In 1915, Mr Stephen J. Jenkins (known as Capt Ste), who was

contractor for the delivery of house coal for the Bishop Rock and Round Island dwellings, was paid 9s 6d, per ton over and above the contract price.

The Bishop Rock mooring buoy came adrift some time during the summer of 1915, and Trinity House had to pay out £2 as salvage remuneration to the persons who recovered it. It came adrift again in 1918, when Mr J. Hicks jnr was paid £7 in settlement for salving it.

At sunset on 24 February 1916 an electrical discharge occurred at Bishop Rock during a thunderstorm. The Principal Keeper reported no apparent damage but detected a strong smell of sulphur inside the tower. The lightning conductor remained in good order.

On 22 November 1917 the light was dimmed and the lower part of the biform lens and burner were discontinued temporarily, and the light in the upper part was reduced by black curtains being placed round the outside the lens.[2] No reason for this was given. However, during the Great War, the Admiralty announced that lighthouses were to be unlit but remain manned. They would come under the jurisdiction of a regional naval officer, 'who would inform individual lighthouses when a convoy was expected and when they should exhibit a light; usually with a reduced range'.[3] So this incident was probably connected to such a convoy.

In December 1917, the fog signal was found to be seriously out of order and that the incandescent oil burner system needed overhauling. But it was not until August 1918 that the cost of £105 for repairs was sanctioned by the Board of Trade.

# CHAPTER TEN

# THE INTER-WAR YEARS

An interesting description of the interior of Bishop Rock lighthouse in the 1920s was given by former AK W. J. Lewis.[1] He commented that very little had changed regarding layout and fittings since the Victorian age.

The exterior gun-metal dog-steps led to the entrance doors also comprising gun-metal, which had stout inside bars to keep them in place when shut. The tower was entered through a small tunnel leading to the base floor under which were the fresh water tanks, lavatory and equipment. Most of this space was taken up by a large central tube.

This tube passes through to the next floor, then gets smaller through the next four rooms before enlarging again in the sitting room. In the large tube are the weights for driving the lens in the lantern. In the larger tube in the sitting room there is also a double chain and some maintenance gear which keeps the lens revolving when the weights are taken off the driving clock for rewinding.

The spiral iron stairs started in the righthand side of the base with rooms leading off it to the left. The magazine room was the first, where the coal, tonite charges and the detonators for the fog signal were stored. The next room housed an oil store with 100-gallon tanks filled with oil for the main navigation light. In here was another coal locker. An additional oil store was on the next floor, as was the kitchen with its large granite mantelpiece above the Cornish range. The circular walls were fitted with food lockers which also formed seats. On the next floor was the bedroom with its built-in washstand and banana-shaped beds hugging the walls. These had drawers underneath in which a keeper's personal items could be kept. The sitting room was on the floor above, and was originally the engine-room. It had a semi-circular table connecting to the weight tube, form seats, an oak bookcase and semi-circular lockers. It was a light room with uninterrupted views. The iron stairs then led to two glass swing doors to the service room.

Everything in this room is designed to increase the weight. There are gun-metal frames to the windows, gun-metal shutters outside, gun-metal cupboards for storing parts for the burners, and some spare diamond and half-diamond glazing for the lantern, oil and air tanks. A tank connected to the oil store by a pipe and semi-rotary pump saves the keepers from having to carry oil in two-gallon cans up the tower in order to fill the incandescent oil burners. On a small table are kept the journals for logging the weather every three hours. Since I left this station a small engine has also been installed in the service room to charge batteries for the radio telephone.

Water tanks were situated around the outer edge of the gallery and were originally for the engines. But their role changed to that of collecting rain water from the roof to be used for anything except drinking water. There was also a winch used for landing heavy items such as coal, oil and water. An iron ladder led to the roof with its copper dome and ventilator with a weather vane.

### THE LIGHT

The light apparatus required attention on and off. In January 1922, new 'Hood' petroleum vapour burners (named after Trinity House Chief Engineer, David Hood who invented them) were installed in the upper and lower apparatus, and the acetylene light had to be re-established in November 1922, for which the keepers were paid 1s 9d per day for night duty while the works were in progress.

The outer glazing was damaged by a storm in 1925 which also extinguished the light and, in 1931, £200 was needed for repairs to the lantern roof, glazing etc. Only three years later, £120 was sanctioned for repairs to the lighting and fog signal apparatus, but this had to be increased to £145. Estimates made in 1938 for the following two years were to include £110 for the overhaul and repair of the lantern framing and glazing.

### FOG SIGNAL

The fog signal, too, needed constant attention and, in 1919, £132 was needed for overhauling the apparatus. £120 expenses were incurred in February 1924 when the Engineer-in-Chief had to repair the fog signal jib etc, and a new dynamo exploder (plunger) was purchased for £12 10s. In March 1925 the Light Committee decided that double-walled autoform mantles should be supplied to all explosive fog signal stations including Bishop Rock.

Due to the holing of a French steamer, *La Touraine* near Bishop Rock, when it ran aground on rocks, the French Chamber of Commerce in London wrote to Trinity House on 21 August 1920 requesting the Bishop Rock fog signal be increased from one report every five minutes, to one every three minutes. This was followed two months later by a letter from the French Ambassador concerning the matter. Trinity House costed this change at an extra £275 p.a., so, unsurprisingly, they declined the request. This met with complaint from the French Chamber of Commerce, but Trinity House remained steadfast.

In August 1930 it was the turn of the German Ambassador to suggest changes to the Bishop Rock fog signal. They wanted a two minute signal, but this was, again, deemed impractical by Trinity House in terms of the type of signal and also the costs involved. The five minute signal now given, supplemented by the use of the Wireless Direction Finding, was considered adequate to meet the needs of navigation.

GENERAL MAINTENANCE

Mainland supplies of coal for both Bishop Rock and Round Island lighthouses were ordered in 1919 at £2 19s 6d a ton. It was delivered to Penzance and from here it was put on a steamer for St Mary's. From November, the men landing it were to be paid 2s a ton as in other districts.

In July 1920, while Trinity House was making an inspection of the lighthouse, the Trinity House Vessel (THV) *Mermaid* made a delivery of stores, oil and water. The Brethren were much struck by what they felt were primitive methods of unloading which had resulted in the first three floors from the entrance door becoming smothered in oil. Each drum was dragged by hand up three flights of steep iron steps. To overcome this problem, they suggested a small tank should be fitted near the entrance into which drums might be emptied. Oil could be pumped by a small hand pump to the upper oil tanks on the third floor. Also, a motor winch should be fitted for the hoisting of the drums as the present hand winch took three or four men. At least four and sometimes five men were hired to assist THV *Mermaid* crew at 12s per day, and sometimes they had to be kept on board several days.

Unspecified repairs to the tower, costing £90, were undertaken in October 1922 and, the following year, Chief Engineer David Hood made an inspection and found it in good condition.

In 1928 repairs were carried out to the lantern roof, and glazing, completed in June, while in 1932, the lighthouse was given an external wire brushing which was to good effect. The water tank around the gallery blistered and had to be repaired in the 1930s, and internal painting took place. It was decided to change the colour scheme from a 'grain colour' to that of light stone. The effect in the living quarters was to brighten it up considerably. The edge of the stone floor on the Magazine landing was found to be badly broken in 1935, caused by the dragging of oil drums up the ladder.

### THE DWELLINGS

In 1929 the dwellings for Bishop Rock and Round Island lighthouses were to be offered to senior keepers. If they declined the offer, the dwelling would be offered to the next senior Assistant Keeper.

It would seem that rubbish from the dwellings was being disposed of over the Garrison wall, which was considered insanitary. The order was given that this practice was to cease and that refuse was either to be transferred to the beach so that the sea could wash it away, or to be buried in the gardens.[2]

The gardens themselves were still in a neglected state, and the Principal Keeper complained that they were too big. In response to this, Trinity House told him to find a tenant for part of them.

By August 1931 the two south end dwellings had developed cracks in the walls suggesting subsidence in the foundations. A survey was carried out and confirmed major work was needed. In September 1932 these major works were given a budget of £300 for 1933/4, during which time the keepers' families would have to be evacuated. PK G. F. Smith, one of those affected, was paid a regulation lodging allowance for the period that his house was vacated in 1933. The repairs were carried out by Mr Trenear.

The planned installation of electric lights in the dwellings was put on hold in January 1937. In the meantime, the engineer was to investigate and report on the possibility of building additional cottages on St Mary's on the Corporation's land.

### THE KEEPERS

The lighthouse keepers continued their work at Peninnis lighthouse. An allowance of 1s 9d a day in 1920 was paid to two keepers during the 24 nights that the oil light was in action when the oil gas light was not available.

Their normal allowance was 1s a day, but in December 1920, the keepers sent Trinity House a petition for an increased allowance of 2s 6d. a day. However, this was refused on the grounds that they attended it while on shore and did not have to attend a Depot each day.

The lighthouse keepers were not to give up their quest for an increase in salary. Just over a year later, in January 1922, Trinity House received a petition from the keepers for a special allowance to meet the 'excessive cost' of living on these lighthouses. This was declined.

Ten years later, in 1932, the keepers made another attempt to supplement their income. In all, there were eight lighthouse keepers on St Mary's for Bishop Rock and Round Island. The four not living in the Trinity House dwellings had to find accommodation elsewhere on the island. These men complained to Trinity House saying that cottages were

hard to obtain, and that they had to pay £1 a week for two rooms with no provision for washing etc. Those with families lived in great discomfort. They further stated that they were forwarding a petition to Trinity House for a special bonus owing to the high costs on Scilly. It would seem that the Board of Trade had acknowledged this and had allowed a special bonus to the Coastguard personnel stationed on the islands. This too was declined.

For cooking purposes in the lighthouse, the keepers had one oil stove with two burners, and an oven with one burner, which would only cook one loaf of bread at a time. Although they worked well, PK Kaye commented that it was not enough for three men cooking independently, and suggested that a three-burner stove and a two-burner oven should replace them. This was unsympathetically received as Trinity House felt a larger stove would cramp the space in the kitchen considerably. However, all was not lost and, by 1923, a Valor Perfection Stove had been installed, which must have eased the culinary logistics.

The first half of 1922 did not go well for two keepers. AK J. Owens resigned in January 1922 after 'unfavourable reports' were made about him, while in June, AK W. L. Williams was severely reprimanded and his name placed at the bottom of the list of AK's (i.e. seventh). He had to forfeit two days' pay and allowances for overstaying his leave without permission on 1 and 2 June.

In late October 1922 SAK Harold Hall arrived at Bishop Rock for duty. He was a mandolin player which he used to play in a spare room

*SAK Harold Hall and his mandolin. Photograph from* LAST OF THE LINE *by Patricia Gumbrell.* COURTESY OF WHITTLES PUBLISHING

above the bedroom (spare when the number of keepers had been reduced from four to three). It was used for recreational purposes such as card playing or listening to the gramophone (a luxury only Bishop Rock had at that time).

Having worked on the Wolf lighthouse, Harold Hall was interested to compare the movement of both lighthouses when struck by heavy seas. He found that Bishop Rock swayed more, which he put down to the tower being taller.

As a SAK, his relief did not last long, and he was posted to the Lizard lighthouse for four weeks. But he found himself returning to Bishop Rock for a two-month spell of duty on 1 January 1923. A fellow keeper, on seeing he was to re-join them, shouted out, 'Make his mandolin fast above the bowline, it doesn't matter if he gets wet'.[3]

Patricia Gumbrell, daughter of Harold Hall, recalled:

> My father once recounted an incident when he and another keeper told a newcomer at the Bishop not to cool the bread he had made on the window sill with the window open. The newcomer knew better, and the consequence was a wave struck the lighthouse pouring water through the open window taking the bread with it. The rest of the night was spent clearing up the mess which went down through the lighthouse.[4]

Hall found his duty on Bishop Rock one of the most exciting times of his career as a lighthouse keeper.

This was due to many occasions of extreme weather e.g. during one storm a clock was knocked off the service room wall and the mercury was shaken out of the revolving optic bath. It was commonly accepted that if the Bishop Tower could stand up to that kind of weather it could take anything.'[5]

During this heavy gale in January 1923, a mechanic had to visit the lighthouse to repair the damage. W. J. Lewis gives a more graphic description of this storm, when keepers shut and bolted the entrance doors and closed the storm shutters on the windows.

> There was a deep thud as the sea struck at our base and crashed along the dog-steps sending a ringing sound right through the tower. The whole structure trembled with the impact – a queer sensation beyond accurate description, and one which calls for strong nerves. It is most often felt when one is sitting and is witnessed by the gentle swinging of cups hanging from a dresser or of a picture on the wall. How amazing that thousands of tons of granite can tremble in such a way without the least defect to foundation, pointing or masonry.

…Suddenly the heavens were split by a flash of lightning. …There followed a loud peal of thunder. A deafening crash struck the sea and was swallowed up rumbling as it made its impetuous flight to the bottom of the ocean.

Suddenly a flash of lightening played on the polished steel band of the lens. The bright bluish-yellow glare was blinding. A fraction of a second seemed like long minutes, and there were startling effects on the polished surfaces before finally the flash passed on down the lightning conductor to the sea below.

The tower rocked in the cradle of the storm while seas fifty or more feet high swept down on it as if from a landslide in the Atlantic. So severe was the sea's onslaught and so cruel the blast that the tower (with little rock to break the impact) seemed to be lifted and shaken unmercifully. Each wave smashed and buried the whole structure in spray causing the light from the lantern to be reflected and to flash just like lightning into the rooms below. The tower seemed almost alive as it danced on its foundations… It was as if all the demons in the universe had gathered at that one lonely spot, screaming their war cry, scoffing at the light which flashed perpetually into their eyes from the lantern, and breathing fear into the imprisoned atmosphere within.

…The sea suddenly struck under the gallery coping with such force that the lens was partially lifted off its mercury bath before dropping back and splashing the mercury like a shower into the lantern. The vibration was so terrific that it took two of us to replace new mantles on the burners as they were shaken off. (These were single-walled mantles and after this experience we were issued with double-walled mantles to put on in the event of another storm).[6]

Apart from the lantern damage, the tower base and equipment were found to be sound.

This storm seems to have affected the keepers quite deeply. Trinity House reported in their minutes that all the keepers nerves were affected due to their experiences over the winter. Indeed, so bad were they that in June, PK Kaye requested a transfer, AK Bowling asked for a transfer on account of his nerves, and AK Richards, who had only been there since January (just in time for the dreadful gales above) asked for a transfer on grounds of a varicolele (?), a threatened rupture, a sprained thigh and other ailments.

W. J. Lewis also revealed how a pipe or cigarette was of great importance to those who smoked, describing it as a friend bringing solace to a lonely occupation. He recalled a time when the relief was overdue

because of bad weather. The PK did not smoke but the others did, and their supply of tobacco ran out. Their frantic searches for 'fag-ends' was watched silently by the PK. Then, one dinner time, each keeper found a whole cigarette by his plate. Offers to buy cigarettes fell on deaf ears, but every dinner time, until the relief could be effected, a cigarette would appear. This kindness was never forgotten.

Sadly, in 1927, the keepers were to lose one of their colleagues. AK T. H. Smith was admitted to the West Cornwall Infirmary for 13 days in early 1927, but he later died. His widow was paid the balance of his wages in March.

In the 1930s one PK was Mr George Smith. Gilbert Pender used to go with Mr Smith's son

> ... to the batteries on the West side of the Garrison with his son Richard (Dick)...Dick as I always called him had a very powerful Aldis lamp for sending Morse at a pre-arranged time, usually 6 or 7pm. We would flash the light towards the Bishop Rock. As soon as we got a reply the day's mail was transmitted by Morse. This was a daily routine and kept Mr Smith up to date with his mail and all the local news.[7]

In August 1928 the keepers requested that their service on an outer rock lighthouse, such as Bishop Rock, should not exceed three years. They had to wait until the 1930s for this request to be met.

Two of the keepers were confirmed in a special service on the lighthouse in August 1936. To conduct this service, the Bishop of Truro, Joseph Hunkin, had to be winched up onto the set-off - and back again afterwards - in his full Church of England regalia from the relief boat. A Bishop landing on a rock of the same name was a rather rare occurrence! He was accompanied by his chaplain, E. C. Seager.

The December 1948 issue of *The Scillonian* reported that 'some years ago', Miss Helen M. Parr and her niece Miss Ethel M. Flindt of Croydon, offered to send £1 a month to be spent at the keepers discretion. PK Bowling and the other keepers decided on a fortnightly boat for the conveyance of fresh food, mail and papers. Captain Ste was to land these goods fortnightly during the summer months for £1, and during the winter months for 27s 6d. The extra cost would be defrayed by three keepers on duty at the time.

Miss Parr died in 1930, closely followed by Miss Flindt in 1931, but the practice was then carried out by Mr Hedley Wright and two friends, Messrs G. A. Taylor of Falmouth and P. L. Grant-Ferris of Warwick. On the death of Capt Ste Jenkins, his son Bert continued these relief visits.

*Bishop Hunkin of Truro ascending up the rope.*
ALK No.B687

*Inside the kitchen.*
GIBSON ARCHIVE

In the 1930s an interesting photograph of the kitchen, shown here, was taken by a member of the well known Gibson family of photographers. On the extreme left is the Cornish range, burnished with black lead. The loop handle in the chimney was for damping. The range appears to be unused as the wireless set has been placed on the hot plate. A thermometer, in the shape of a lighthouse, is on top of the wireless. To the right of the wireless is its speaker, sitting on top of the Library Box. This box was supplied to most rock lighthouses by the British Sailor's Society, of London and Carnegie Libraries for the Trinity House Service.

The most prominent piece of furniture in the room is the dresser, which looks slightly curved to fit the circular walls. Although not very clear to see, there are two pairs of scissors hanging on the lefthand side, while books fill the two shelves. Beneath these shelves, the foolscap-sized books look like station documents, such as the Visitor Book and SAK Book.

The clock above the dresser show the time as 12 o'clock. Assuming the clock had not stopped, this indicates either midday or midnight. The former is more likely as natural light is in evidence, and it would be a more usual time for a photographer to visit!

A framed chart is hanging on the wall to the right of the dresser. It illustrates the component parts of the Hood incandescent oil burner, otherwise known as the petroleum vapour burner. These charts were issued to every station with this type of burner. The smaller frame below hold a sunrise and sunset chart. This was important because the whole procedure of lighting up took about 30 minutes, taking into account the warming up of the burner, taking down the lantern curtains, lighting the lamp etc. The light had to be exhibited 20 minutes before sunset, and was extinguished 20 minutes after sunrise.

Not clearly visible is a curved, fitted bench under the plaques, while the captain's chair in the centre was a standard issue.

To the right of the photograph is the weight tube, showing the inspection door with brass handle and locking pin.

The floral patterned tablecloth was a design supplied to many lighthouses, and was of a dark brown or red hue. It matched the brown lino and brown-painted walls. On the table itself is a book entitled Oil and Fog Books. The Principal Keeper or Keeper-in-Charge had to keep an exact account of the number of hours a fog signal was in use and the consumables used such as fuel oil, lubricating oil, explosive charges and detonators. He also had to record fuel oil used for the lamps on the station, both navigation and domestic lamps, as well as fuel used for the refrigerators, engines and compressors. The quantities used, to the nearest pint, quart or gill had to be accounted for, although allowances were made for spillages during deliveries etc. Such records were used to schedule the next deliveries, and also prevented misuse of stores.

Another book is on the table - probably the Correspondence Book in which the Principal Keeper or Keeper-in-Charge wrote reports about the movements of personnel, the need for any repairs, or the replacement of stores and equipment.[8]

## THE RELIEFS

The period of reliefs changed in the 1930s. At a meeting of Whitley Council on 24 September 1931, it was decided that Bishop Rock, along with Wolf Rock, Longships and Smalls (off the Pembrokeshire coast) lighthouses should be made 3-year stations.

Winter months were times of difficult reliefs; for example, on 12 February 1919 the relief boat brought ashore AK Warder in exceptionally rough weather. For this, the boatman was paid £2 7s in addition to his usual £3 10s.

Getting on and off the lighthouse did not hold great appeal for many keepers and may be why, in June 1919, Trinity House received a petition from PK H. E. Howgego at Bull Point lighthouse on the North Devon coast, asking them not to transfer him to Bishop Rock but to send him to the Channel Islands Station instead! They refused to comply with his request.

In 1921 AK W. J. Lewis, mentioned above, began his first appointment at Bishop Rock. He was to serve 45 years as a lighthouse keeper on various land and rock stations. Recalling his memories in his book *Ceaseless Vigil*, the very first chapter opens with Bishop Rock, and he describes his first glance of the lighthouse as a 'grim sentinel'. Of the relief, he describes first hand how a man was winched up onto the lighthouse:

> I placed my foot in a bowling and grasped the rope. The signal was given to heave away, and slowly I was hauled from the boat. The hauling-off line which was made fast to the main rope was cautiously released by one of the boatmen who was taking great care not to let it go too quickly. A mistake here and I would swing into the base of the tower with a crash. I left the boat at a slant and was gradually hauled in until finally I reached the set-off.[9]

The returning keeper and his belongings then were lowered into the boat for his return to St Mary's.

> The ropes were immediately cast off from the boat and hauled back on the set-off to be stowed later in the base of the tower. The Jack Roll was dismantled and the various parts hauled up from the set-off. The main winch rope was hauled up and coiled on the gallery.[10]

In 1920 the lifeboat station on St Agnes was closed. Richard Lethbridge, author of *Behind the Eyebrows*, explains why. Apparently, shortly before closure, a lighthouse keeper had fallen ill and needed to be taken ashore. The St Agnes lifeboat *Charles Deere James II* was launched and was well on its way to Bishop Rock before the St Mary's crew were aware of the incident. They hastily launched their own craft, the motor-powered *Elsie*. Suffice to say that the *Elsie* arrived at the Rock first and the sick keeper was removed to St Mary's. The RNLI decided that motor-power was greatly beneficial and, largely because of this incident, the St Agnes station was dispensed with.

This may be the incident recorded in Trinity House records, for 8 March 1920. They received a claim from the RNLI for £56 7s in respect of a poorly AK Glendener being brought ashore. But Trinity House were reluctant to pay, claiming that no such callout had been made to the lifeboats. However, they were prepared to give £8 payable under contract for one relief boat trip, and this to be confined to the lifeboat which actually brought the keeper ashore. They then increased this to £15. But the Board of Trade, who appears to have been more sympathetic, sanctioned the whole amount.

Israel Hicks retired as relief boatman in 1919 and, in November, he applied to Trinity House for a bonus on retirement, but this was declined.

In February 1920 Capt Stephen (Ste) Jenkins and his son Albert (Bert) (and later, grandson Stephen Roy) took over the relief for Bishop Rock and Round Island lighthouses from St Mary's. They were paid:

Bishop Rock at £8 per trip
   (£4 per unsuccessful trip)
Round Island at £8 per trip

Capt Ste Jenkins' contract was renewed annually and, despite requests from Trinity House, he would not reduce his rates. As no other offer was obtained to do the work, they had to agree to the £8 per trip. For some reason, in 1932, Capt Ste Jenkins reduced his rates for the reliefs to:

Bishop Rock at £5 per trip
   (£2 10s per unsuccessful trip)
Round Island  at £4 per trip
   (£2 per unsuccessful trip)

The following year, he wrote to Trinity House offering to make no charge for unsuccessful trips, whether relief or special and, not surprisingly, this was accepted. But in August 1933, Capt Ste retired as boatman, and a fresh contract was entered into with his son Bert at the same rates. Should extra men be needed in addition to his crew of three, for handling heavy stores, an extra sum of £1 a man would be paid. In 1937, the reliefs continued, but with a crew of 3 men only in the twin-engined relief boat.

The 1930s saw the start of film companies and publishers obtaining permission from Trinity House, to film various aspects of Bishop Rock lighthouse, such as Rayant Pictures Ltd, the BBC, *Evening Post* and *Picture Post*.

*Bishop Rock lighthouse in the 1940s.* FOX PHOTOS LTD, COURTESY ALK

CHAPTER ELEVEN
# SECOND WORLD WAR

A sense of vulnerability may well have been experienced by lighthouse keepers on Bishop Rock during the Second World War. The Isles of Scilly played its part in the war and, as on the mainland, did not escape enemy action. German bombs were dropped, and their low flying enemy aircraft meant civilians were susceptible to gunfire. These resulted in major damage, casualties and fatalities.

Trinity House did not escape either, as some of their buildings in London were destroyed by fire due to enemy action on 29 December 1940.

But throughout it all, maintenance and manning of the lighthouse had to continue, and various recommendations were implemented as a direct result of war, as seen below.

Steps were taken in 1940 to paint the words LIGHTHOUSE SERVICE on the sides of lighthouse tenders and relief boats. The risk from enemy action while keepers were being taken to and from duty in a Trinity House tender or relief boat was given further recognition by the Ministry of Defence Transport when they were paid a War Risk Allowance with effect from 1 April 1942.

Lighthouses were often casualties of enemy action and the Wolf Rock and Longships lighthouses were no exception. For example, the Longships lighthouse off Lands End was hit by enemy bombs on Friday 1 August 1941 and resulted in extensive damage to the fog signal plant and electric generators, with both the light and fog signal being rendered useless. A triple reed horn fog signal and a petroleum vapour burner light were installed as an interim measure. Luckily, no keepers were injured, despite their quarters being slightly affected, and they were evacuated in lifeboats. As a result of this episode, enquiries were made among the rock lighthouse keepers, including those at Bishop Rock, as to whether they wanted defensive armaments, but they declined. Tragically, at St Catherine's lighthouse on the Isle of Wight, three keepers were killed when a bomb was dropped onto the building.

Peninnis lighthouse also suffered attacks in April 1941, but miraculously escaped damage as the bombers missed their target. It was hit again on 7 June and this time, the keepers suggested a sandbag shelter could be provided for them. But, for some reason, Trinity House would not agree to this. The wireless communications post on Peninnis was targeted by the Germans and was eventually destroyed, so it is fortunate that the nearby lighthouse stayed intact.

Bishop Rock lighthouse never did get bombed. It was a useful navigation aid from the air as well as the sea, for enemies as well as the British. For example, on 20 May 1942, a German aircraft flew low over the Coastguard Station, located the lighthouse and then continued on its way.[1]

On 25 September 1940 the Trinity House Chief Engineer sent in a report outlining a scheme for Radio Telephone at Bishop Rock, Wolf Rock, Round Island and Longships lighthouses. This included communication through the Lands End Coast Radio Station but with a supplementary shore station at Sennen Coastguard Lookout. This would be carried out as a charge against the Admiralty. Trinity House approved the scheme, and the keepers were sent to the Marconi Station for training in their use.

Marconi Wireless Telegraph Co. Ltd sent Trinity House tenders in July 1941 for the supply and installation of radio telephone equipment at both Bishop Rock (£502) and Round Island (£542) lighthouses, plus the services of an erecting engineer. These were accepted.[2] At the end of the war, Trinity House recommended they should be retained permanently.

In the 1940s the Mission to Seamen had provided broadcast receiver sets at rock lighthouses, including Bishop Rock, and Trinity House decided they would take them over themselves on 1 August 1945.

THE LIGHT

The lantern glazing was overhauled and re-conditioned in 1941 at a cost of £115. On 6 March the following year, Trinity House approved the engineer's recommendation that an electric lamp should be installed in the lower tier of the lighting apparatus, to be operated from the Radio Transmitter (R/T) batteries, at a cost of £45. This lamp was used instead of the petroleum vapour burner, and with a dim mantle for exhibition of the light in clear weather. This dimming of the light was presumably for war purposes; as with the Great War, all navigation lights around the islands were extinguished except for aiding convoys. Approval was given in October 1941 for Bishop Rock, Round Island and Peninnis lighthouses to exhibit their lights when necessary for either assisting air rescue craft or for aiding launches back to harbour rather than relying upon dead reckoning.

## General Maintenance

The mooring buoy became something of a nuisance during this period. It had come adrift again in March 1940, and Trinity House was compelled to make a payment of £20 in May to the Belgian trawler *Gralie Gods* for its recovery, which had been heavy and time consuming work. It was completely lost in July 1941 and a new one had to be laid. Just over two years later, the mooring buoy became adrift again, and it was recovered undamaged from Shipman Head just off Bryher. But the chains and sinker had to be written off as lost. In September 1944, the disappearance of the mooring buoy meant yet another replacement.

The Duchy of Cornwall informed Trinity House in May 1940, that linking the four dwellings to the new drains had cost £2 10s 4d and they requested payment. The rent was also increased from £10 to £18 p.a. from 24 June 1940. In September, Trinity House approved the building of two concrete shelters at the lighthouse dwellings, while in December, they were fitted out with exchange telephones, initially for the duration of the war, but they were retained permanently as a service necessary for peace time. Camouflage painting of the dwellings took place at the expense of Naval Funds in early 1941 and was undertaken by Colenso & Co.

On 1 January 1943, the painting gratuities, introduced in 1920, were doubled as a war time measure. At the close of the war, both Bishop Rock and Eddystone lighthouses were repointed and overhauled at a cost of £400.

## The Keepers

In 1939 the Board of Trade purchased an emergency stock of foodstuffs for keepers on rock lighthouses and light vessels at a cost of £560. The money was to be recoverable from those who bought the stock; however, for some reason, many keepers were reluctant to purchase these goods; whether the Corporation ever recovered its costs is not known!

As a guard against the reduction of staff through enemy action, it was recommended in April 1941 that an additional keeper should be stationed at rock lighthouses as it would not be practical, with the existing staff of three keepers, for the remaining two (or possibly one) keepers to work the landing gear at Bishop Rock, Wolf Rock, Eddystone and Longships lighthouses. In other words, this meant the employment of four keepers plus two additional ones for relief.

In September 1942 the keepers narrowly escaped an additional duty. The Admiralty's Naval Meteorological Branch was given permission to observe the swell at Bishop Rock, and to send a representative to the keepers to instruct them in how to implement the scheme. The Admiralty was asked to pay 6d per meteorological observation for so long as the observations of 'SWELL' were required to be made at the lighthouse on their behalf. However, the Admiralty declined this and went elsewhere. In 1944 they repeated their request which, again, was later withdrawn.

The SAK's period of duty on Bishop Rock, Wolf Rock, Longships, Smalls and Eddystone lighthouses changed from June 1943. This was to avoid them working excessive periods on rock lighthouses by bringing them ashore after two months and exchanging stations with a SAK serving at a shore station.

The Director of Naval Intelligence became concerned that messages transmitted from Bishop Rock could be intercepted by the enemy. All lighthouses and light vessels were allowed to use plain English only on Radio Transmissions. The set at Bishop Rock was a Marconi PV5/R59 working on 1650 Kc/s. In 1944 it was suggested, therefore, that messages transmitted from the lighthouse should be in code and, if they were unable to use an existing one, they could perhaps devise one. But it was pointed out to the Director that care had been taken to preserve the non-belligerent nature of lighthouses, and so this project was abandoned.

THE RELIEFS

In March 1940 Bert Jenkins was informed by Trinity House that his relief work could continue for the duration of the war without his having to re-apply each year and, in November 1940, approval was given to meet his request for increased relief payments of £7 for Bishop Rock and £5 for Round Island. They also felt that protection on his boat against machine gun fire was not practicable.

The call-up of lighthouse personnel was always of concern as replacements were hard to find. In 1942 Trinity House recommended that the Ministry of Labour and National Service and the Ministry of War Transport be informed of the unsuccessful result of the efforts made to obtain a substitute to carry on the relief and boat work for Bishop Rock and Round Island lighthouses if the present contractor was called up. They also felt that the Trinity House Penzance District tender would encounter difficulties if it was called upon to do the relief duty. Therefore they requested that the call-up of Bert Jenkins be deferred.

In July 1942 Pilot Guy expressed an interest in taking on the relief duty, so Bert Jenkins took him out to teach him the procedures. But it was only a couple of weeks later that Pilot Guy withdrew his offer so, in August 1943, Trinity House asked for a further period of deferment. In fact, a replacement was never found.

Bishop Rock lighthouse survived the war unscathed, much to the relief of all concerned and, slowly, life on the Isles returned to a peacetime state.

RELIEF DAY, BISHOP LIGHTHOUSE . No 100 .

*A bird's eye view of the relief.* GIBSON ARCHIVE

*Relief for AK Duff on 14 February 1948.* FOX PHOTOS LTD, COURTESY ALK

# CHAPTER TWELVE

# 1946 TO 1973

The well-documented saga of Edward Ward's incarceration in Bishop Rock lighthouse began in November 1946 when Trinity House gave permission for two BBC representatives to visit either Bishop Rock or Round Island, with a view to a live broadcast in the BBC Christmas 'Round-up' programme. The former lighthouse was chosen, and the BBC was given permission for commentator Edward Ward, and engineer Stanley Cooms to remain there from 19 to 26 December, using the Trinity House transmitter at Lands End for the purpose.

The script for the programme was approved by Trinity House in mid-December, but part of it was re-written by the keepers as they felt it was not very good. A practice run took place in the early hours of Christmas Eve which was recorded in case there was a technical problem with the live broadcast. Coombs and Ward slept in the spare top bunks where headroom was very limited, and bumping one's head on the granite ceiling was a consequence of forgetting this.[1]

Having been taken out to the lighthouse by Bert Jenkins and his son Roy in their boat *Verona*, the two BBC men never thought they would be there for New Year and beyond! But the weather turned, bringing with it gale force winds and turbulent seas, and their week-long stay turned into four long weeks. With them they had taken various provisions, supplied by the BBC, including a turkey and a Christmas pudding, which they shared with the keepers.

The BBC asked that St Mary's lifeboat *Cunard* and crew make attempts to remove Ward and Cooms from the lighthouse, which they did with the assistance of Bert Jenkins and his team, but to no avail. On 2 January 1947, Trinity House gave the BBC permission for Edward Ward to give a two minute broadcast on that evening's 9 o'clock news, 'an undertaking having been given verbally by the BBC that the wording of the broadcast will in no way be derogatory to the Trinity House Service.'[2]

The broadcasts on both Christmas Day and 2 January took place in the living quarters where the keepers had to use blankets to create a makeshift tent to alleviate the hollow sound of the tower.

Another attempt later in January by St Mary's lifeboat, accompanied

by Bert Jenkins, was successful. The lifeboat crew were taking food rations out to the lighthouse as the 'iron rations' were being consumed and the keepers' own food supplies were dwindling with the two extra men to feed. The sea was still rough but a successful attempt was made to winch the men off from the doorway higher up than the set-off. Richard Lethbridge, one of the lifeboat crewmen, described how an emergency bottle of cherry brandy was opened aboard the lifeboat as a 'celebration', which was greatly appreciated.

In an article written by Edward Ward for *Picture Post* magazine, he gave an insight into how the lighthouse keepers of this time occupied themselves when not on duty or sleeping; for example, SAK Jack Beale, made rope-soled slippers while the others made rugs.

He also gave details of the watch hours: 'one man is on duty from midnight to 4 a.m., the next from 4 until 9. Then from 9 to 1, 1 to 7, and 7 to midnight again.'[5]

While Ward and Coombs were in the lighthouse, much media

attention was being generated. The keepers' wives were constantly receiving telephone calls from the press, not only asking where Bishop Rock was, but asking whether Ward and Coombs would have a bedroom each, would they have servants to wait on them, and were there any women living in the lighthouse?[4]

Following on from this saga, Trinity House was to claim a portion of the costs of radio telegrams sent by Ward and Coombs during their stay in the lighthouse. They also made a claim against the BBC to compensate them for the sum of £43 3s 1d paid to the Marconi Wireless Telegraph Co. Ltd for the special re-tuning of the Bishop Rock transmitter and receiver in connection with the BBC 'Round Up' programme.

## THE LIGHT

The 1950s saw various repairs to the lantern and lighting apparatus; for example, £326 3s 6d was spent in 1950 on new lantern glazing and pipework, while in 1957, £545 6s 5d was needed, amongst other things, for the adjustment of the lens clock and governor, and renewal of the complete oil pipe line and sections of the flue pipe.

*The rescue of Edward Ward and Stanley Cooms.* FOX PHOTOS LTD, COURTESY ALK

In early 1972 the Board approved the engineer's proposal for a major modernisation of the light at Bishop Rock the following year, converting it from a paraffin vapour burner to an incandescent electric filament lamp. Although not involving any change in the existing character of the light, it increased the intensity of the main light from 720,000 candelas (nominal range 25 miles) to 2,600,000 candelas (nominal range 29 miles) with an emergency light of 88,000 candelas (nominal range 19 miles) and a decrease in the existing flash length of 0.7 second to 0.3 second for the main light and 0.33 second for the emergency light. The costs of modernisation were estimated at £131,200.[5]

Approval was given in May 1973, to install fuel tanks and piping etc, make good the electric drive to the optic, and the electrification of the light. This was at an estimated cost of £17,500, of which £8,688 had already been sanctioned. A few months later, in September, a quotation was accepted from Renold Ltd for six Dual Variable Speed Optic Drives required for electrification of optics at Alderney, Beachy Head, Lynmouth Foreland, Trevose, St Mary's (Peninnis) and Bishop Rock lighthouses, costing £3,645.30.

Work progressed well on these plans during the latter part of 1973 and, on 13 December, the new light of increased intensity with its nominal range of 29 miles was successfully brought into operation at Bishop Rock lighthouse.

### FOG SIGNAL

As ever, the fog signal also needed maintenance during these years. Then, in January 1969, a modernisation scheme was approved, for the installation of a Supertyfon (compressed air) fog signal for Bishop Rock. Fog signal listening trials were carried out off Dungeness on 25 September and 11 October 1972 and a report was sent to Trinity House discussing possible alternatives for fog signals at both Bishop Rock and Beachy Head. Trinity House recommended that the Supertyfon fog signal to be installed should have a characteristic of Morse (N) every 90 seconds thus:

Blast 4.5 seconds, Silent 2.0 seconds
Blast 1.5 seconds, Silent 82 seconds

### COMMUNICATIONS

Methods of communication also changed. On 1 May 1947, the Ministry of Supply successfully requested that facilities be approved to install radio transmission and receiving apparatus at Bishop Rock lighthouse in connection with Supersonic Model tests to be carried out off the Isles of Scilly. The total cost of the renewal and fitment of the radio transmitting batteries amounted to £265 4s 11d by 1953. Six years later, six more receivers were bought for the lighthouse at a cost of £7 14s.

This equipment was tested two or three times daily by the keepers with the nearest Coastal Radio Station, a Coastguard Station or light station. Several stations would undertake the tests at the same time, giving an opportunity for keepers to exchange news. For example, the Gwennap Head Coastguard at Land's End would undertake a test with Bishop Rock, Round Island, Longships, Wolf Rock and Eddystone lighthouses, and Seven Stones lightship.[6] This change in communications must have been of some significance to keepers who could now talk to other people rather than just each other.

In 1964 Trinity House decided that radar beacons were to be fitted at Bishop Rock lighthouse in accordance with the recommendations of the Working Party and Technical Committee who had investigated the matter the year before. The Tol Pedn Penwith Coastguard Station at Gwennap Head was to be the Base Station for Radio Transmitter communication with Bishop Rock, Round Island, Longships, Wolf Rock and Eddystone lighthouses and the Seven Stones light vessel.

Four years later, in September 1969, VHF Radio Telephone links were installed at Bishop Rock.

GENERAL MAINTENANCE

Former AK Tony Thomas (1945-48) described how the copper plated roof on the lighthouse became pitted when the fog signal explosive went off. This roof had to be maintained regularly and, during the 1940s, this was done by Leonard Prowse of Penzance.

It would seem that Mr Prowse did not always enjoy his rock lighthouse experience. In the autumn of 1947, he was sent to Bishop Rock to repair the roof but became incapacitated. A national newspaper reported his indisposition, and described how he was taken off by the relief boat five days later. It has to be said that not many people would relish the thought of undertaking this work. To climb out onto the roof from the gallery with the rocks and swirling sea beneath would induce varying degrees of vertigo in most people, and be a major handicap in executing the necessary maintenance.

The lighthouse underwent repointing in 1951, and A. Taylor & Son were paid £260 6d for this task.

A mishap occurred in 1960 when the Schermuly Pistol Rocket Apparatus (a rocket system to fire a line from land/lighthouse to a boat from a small hand held pistol) was lost from the lighthouse and had to be written off. It was replaced at an estimated cost of £37 17s 6d less 10%.

The sum of £11,400 was allocated for four new keepers' dwellings at St Mary's; this had increased to £18,800 by 1950. The existing keepers dwellings also underwent alterations. For example, the St Mary's (Scilly) Electricity Supply Co. Ltd installed electricity in all four houses in the 1950s and, in 1958, a licence was granted by the Duchy of Cornwall for the laying of a water main to each house. Further items, including new cookers and fireplaces were also fitted and, by 1962, the total cost of refurbishing the dwellings had reached £7,992 8s 6d. It was while this work was being carried out that the Clerk to the Council of the Isles of Scilly successfully requested that the workmen construct a water tank on the Garrison on a repayment basis.

A new lease between Trinity House and the Duchy of Cornwall, for the four keepers' dwellings and land, had been sealed in May 1954 while, the following year, due to escalating costs, the plan for the new houses was abandoned.

The Department of Botany requested permission to install an

additional pollen-trapping apparatus at the lighthouse which would be operated by a $1/8$ h.p. electric motor. Trinity House approved this as long as the keepers were willing to co-operate.

New fuel oil storage tanks were ordered for the lighthouse in 1972 from Braby Group Ltd plus ancillary equipment at a cost of £8,688.

THE KEEPERS

Former AK Tony Thomas detailed some of the food rations he and his colleagues had. Each keeper cooked every third day for them all, but he baked his own bread. The yeast was fresh and kept in a Kilner jar which was placed in a water tank to keep cool as there were no fridges in the 1940s (although the idea was first mooted by Trinity House in 1947). A special concession for keepers was pure white flour. Post-war rationing was still in hand and poorer quality flour was more commonly available.

As well as dried food, the men took out a big piece of beef and some mutton fat. The meat was cut into cubes and cooked for about 4-5 hours and then sealed with the fat. This was stored in the white stone Dundee marmalade jars of that period, and could be kept for 4-5 months. This, together with butter beans and potatoes, was their staple diet, and the cooking was done on an old Cornish range. No fishing to supplement their diet was undertaken during Mr Thomas's time.

Keepers were allowed 140 or so gallons of drinking water a month. This, together with oil and coal, was brought to the lighthouse by the Trinity House District Tender, *Satellite*. The water collected from the roof in large water tanks was for cleaning only as it was contaminated with copper.

Once or twice, when weather prevented a relief taking place for a long period of time, Mr Thomas found himself on a diet of bully beef and hardtack biscuits.

Cleaning was carried out regularly before a relief was effected, and the first job was to get out on to the top of the lighthouse with a brush to sweep the chimney. From the gallery, one man had to climb a ladder which jutted out and on to the top. A rope was then put down the chimney with the brush attached. This vertiginous job, like the roof repairs described above, was not for the faint-hearted, but Mr Thomas said it was a job he didn't mind doing!

During their spare time, Mr Thomas did carpentry and Jack Beale made rope-bottomed slippers, as witnessed by Edward Ward, out of the landing rope which had to be discarded after being used three or four times. Some keepers also made rag mats.

However, in 1951, one keeper found a novel way of keeping himself occupied. He was the proud owner of a bicycle which was in need of some attention, so he arranged for the machine to be taken out to the lighthouse

on one of his turns of duty so that he could work on it when time permitted. But before he could start repairs, the delivery of coal, oil and water arrived, and he was compelled to hang his bicycle outside the tower to keep it out of everyone's way. The boatloads of visitors brought out to watch this delivery could not fail to see this spectacle, and soon news spread throughout the island visitor population that the lighthouse contained a mad keeper who kept his bicycle there.[7]

*AK Duff being relieved on 14 February 1948.* FOX PHOTOS LTD, COURTESY ALK

Another incident involved a keeper whose wife sent out a life-size female dummy as a surprise gift. The keeper had fun pretending to canoodle with the 'lady' in front of the tripper boats![8]

Mr Thomas also remembers the Thompsons from St Mary's bringing out day trippers with the mail in their boats.

In early February 1948 the keepers found themselves on iron rations (the emergency rations used when reliefs could not be effected) due to heavy storms. However, the St Mary's lifeboat, out on a practice trip, managed to get some fresh food to the keepers and, on 14th, they were taken off. But news of their incarceration on the tower reached the press which did not please them. *The Times* reported that SAK Victor Brading and two other keepers had been on the lighthouse for 101 days, the longest period for 20 years, due to the storms. 'It seems the lighthouse keepers have decided they have had enough publicity, and now wish to carry on their lonely way without any more comments and admiration concerning their courageous life'.[9]

Various changes occurred in the lives of the keepers too. In June 1951, the standard reserve provisions at Bishop Rock, Wolf Rock and Longships lighthouses were improved due to the long periods of 'overdue' which occurred at these stations.

Rock allowances documented for the early 1950s were:

Victualling Allowance – 4s each day to each keeper;

House Allowance – 4s 6d a day to two AK's (PK and one AK live in official dwellings);

Wireless Telephone (chargeable to Electrical Communications) – 4d a day PK, 3d a day AK's;

Rock Allowance – each keeper received 2s 6d a day.

From 1 July 1953 keepers living with their families on the islands (and not the mainland) were paid an additional allowance of 5s a week.

In March 1953 the Superintendent in Penzance sent Trinity House reports about the failure of the fog signal between 0435 and 0745 on 20 February, and also the stoppage of the lens on 24 February. As a consequence, one keeper was severely reprimanded for his failure to report the stoppage of the lens, and another was dismissed the service for his part in putting the fog signal out of action.

A touch of luxury arrived for the keepers when, in July 1953, Trinity House decided to spend £629 on three 'Electrolux Type' L 150 kerosene-operated refrigerators for each lighthouse at Bishop Rock, Wolf Rock, Longships, Eddystone and Plymouth Breakwater lighthouses. For each station, they paid £100 16s for three refrigerators plus £25 to install them. £15 per station was allowed for maintenance each year.

Some time later, Electrolux advertised their fridges in a national

*Delivery of a van to a keeper at the lighthouse.*
GIBSON ARCHIVE

magazine, mentioning they had also been installed at Bishop Rock, complete with a photograph. They obviously thought it was a good selling point.

During the 1960s another luxury was introduced. The Bishop Rock keepers were given a television, the first lighthouse to get one.[10]

A rather strange delivery took place at Bishop Rock in 1963. Keeper George Peacock had bought a van from Arthur Richards, a car salesman from St Austell in Cornwall. Mr Richards and the car were taken out to the lighthouse by Benny and David Badcock in their motor launch, *Guiding Star*[11] for Mr Peacock to admire while he was on duty!

Three keepers in 1969 nearly missed a Christmas at home when bad weather struck. They were stranded on the lighthouse for nearly a week due to bad weather. However, on 23 December, the weather abated so that George and Michael Hicks were able to relieve the men in their motor launch, *Swordfish*. It did mean, of course, that the outgoing keepers could not have an unscheduled Christmas on land! Accompanying them out to the lighthouse was Rev W. Rowett who gave them carol sheets to use on Christmas morning.[12]

The lighthouse continued to be affected by bad weather. After another storm, it was reported that the remains of a fisherman's pot and some rope were found hanging from the lighthouse about 70 feet up.

From an account by Tony Parker, who spent time interviewing and living with lighthouse keepers in the early 1970s, the hours of duty had changed slightly. In the 1970s, he describes them as midnight to 4am, 4am to 12 noon, 12 noon to 4pm, 4pm to 8pm and 8pm to midnight. The keepers, as was the usual practice, did them in rotation.

*A mailsack is winched up to the lighthouse from* LILY OF LAGUNA, *while Gee Hicks (centre) holds her steady.*
COURTESY JEREMY RESEIGH WATTS AND F. A. WEBB

He also recorded the supplies one keeper had for his two-month stretch on the rock lighthouse. It was probably typical of many keepers during the 1970s:

2 lbs tea; 1 box (72) tea-bags; 2 jars (18 oz each) instant coffee; 6 large tins powdered milk; 16 lbs sugar; 4 lbs butter; 2 lbs margarine; 1$^1$/$_2$ lbs cooking fat; 2 uncut loaves; 6 lbs plain flour; 4 lbs self-raising flour; 56 lbs potatoes; 26 lbs carrots; 2 large cabbage; 2 $^1$/$_2$ lbs fresh tomatoes; 4 lbs cheddar cheese; 24 Oxo cubes; 2 lbs rice; 8 lbs jam; 4 lbs marmalade; 8 pkts cracker biscuits; 4 lbs bacon; 24 eggs; 3 pkts soap powder (large); 4 tablets toilet soap; 8 toilet rolls; 4 tubes toothpaste; 8 pkts sweet biscuits; 1 tube mustard; 2 jars pickle; 4 pkts cereal; 2 boxes (12 assorted) cheese spread; 4 lbs onions; 24 tins peas; 24 tins broad beans; 24 tins baked beans; 24 tins carrots; 2 lbs fresh sausages; 12 tins sausages; 36 assorted tins spaghetti; macaroni, snacks etc; 6 tins corned beef; 12 tins minced beef; 24 tins stewing steak; 6 tins plums; 6 tins pineapple; 6 tins strawberries; 6 tins fruit salad; 5 lbs cooking apples; 5 lbs eating apples; 2 tins syrup (2 lbs); 6 tins luncheon meat; 12 small bars chocolate; 18 boxes matches; 1,000 cigarettes; 12 asst tins soup; 12 tins tomatoes; 12 oranges; 6 unripe grapefruit; 1 drum salt; 1 drum pepper; 2 bottles sauce; 2 lbs fresh steak; 4 lamb chops.[13]

Quantities of fresh produce were limited for obvious reasons, and the men continued to bake their own bread.

The same keeper also gave details of the clothing and personal items he brought with him:

4 pairs of underpants, 4 vests, 2 pairs of pyjamas, 6 pairs of socks, 4 working shirts, 2 nice shirts, 2 pullovers, 1 pair working trousers, 2 pairs of comfortable casual trousers, 12 handkerchiefs, 1 light jacket, 1 pair of

slippers, 2 towels, 1 facecloth, 1 hairbrush, 1 comb, 1 razor, shaving-soap, 1 bottle of hair shampoo, 3 packets of razor blades, a tin of lighter fuel, a packet of throat pastilles, a nail file, a pair of toenail cutters, a sponge bag.[14]

## THE RELIEFS

The reliefs underwent a change too. Bert Jenkins died suddenly on Easter Monday in 1952 and his son, Roy took over the Trinity House contract. In May, his rates for the relief trips were approved:

Bishop Rock relief and extra trip at £10 per trip
Round Island relief and extra trip at £8 per trip

But tragedy struck the Jenkins family on 18 August 1952. Roy Jenkins, together with his uncle, John Clare Jenkins, died in an accident while on a fishing trip in their boat *Verona* (the relief boat) near the Crim Rocks. The Bishop Rock keepers reported seeing them at 10.30am off the Crim Rocks.

As a consequence, on 10 September, Mr George (Gee) Hicks, of St Mary's stepped in. On 26 September, Trinity House recommended that an agreement be entered into with him on the same terms as the late Roy Jenkins, plus an allowance of £1 per month for additional responsibilities in connection with stores and equipment in transit to and from the lighthouses. This was approved and a draft agreement was drawn up in November 1952. George Hicks undertook the reliefs with his brother Lloyd (for about 11 years) and his son Mike. As well as the reliefs, they took out coal to the lighthouses for the Rayburn stoves in their boat *Swordfish*. Occasionally, the Hicks had to undertake relief trips to the Seven Stones light vessel and also to Wolf Rock lighthouse when the relief from Penzance was unable to attend. The boat *Lily of Laguna* was also used to deliver mail to the lighthouse keepers.[15]

From St Mary's, the Hickses judged whether a relief was possible if certain rocks remained uncovered. If waves were washing over them, it was too rough. It was also considered too rough if the waves reached the set-off 40 feet up - it would be too dangerous for the men to land on it.

Depending on the weather and tides, the relief could take between 50 minutes and 2 hours, usually travelling at 7 knots. Mike Hicks reckoned that they could get within about three yards of the rock, which was preferred, as goods were better off being lifted straight up rather than at an angle.

New rates for the boat hire with George Hicks were fixed in May 1964:
Bishop Rock - from £10 to £14 per trip
Round Island - from £8 to £10 per trip.

For his book *Lighthouse*, Tony Parker interviewed a relief boatmen in about the late 1960s, for either Bishop Rock or the Longships lighthouse (he declined to identify which one), and went out on a relief trip with him. He described getting a keeper onto the lighthouse:

> You have to work like a team with them. When the keeper in the boat has got into the harness on the rope, they start winding him up and you have to keep the boat the right distance away from the tower. The right distance is when the rope is tight but not taut, so you have to be all the time keeping your eye on it and where your boat is. If you were to let the sea push you too far away from the tower, the rope could snap and the man would fall in the sea; on the other hand if you're carried too close in, the rope gets loose and the man would swing in against the tower and hit it and perhaps break his back.
>
> As he gets higher up the rope you have to move closer in towards the tower so the keeper can be caught hold of and pulled on by the others.[16]

The procedure was reversed for a keeper coming off the tower into the boat.

## HELICOPTERS

The first mention of using helicopters was in March 1968, when it was decided to investigate their use for personnel reliefs at selected stations on the west coast of England for an experimental period. This was still under discussion in October when the Helicopter sub-committee met and recommended granting approval to proceed with a six-month experiment resulting from an offer made to them in June by Autair Ltd. The costs incurred would be £17,600. But a decision was deferred for the Light Committee to consider

Discussions about helicopter experiments continued and, in March 1969, it was finally recommended by the Light Committee that Bristow Helicopters Ltd should provide the service of a Wessex '60' Helicopter to effect the reliefs of west coast lighthouses for an experimental period of six months, at a rate of £3,000 per month, inclusive of 15 flying hours.

As £50,000 had been provided for this in estimates for 1969-70, this was agreed, and the first helicopter experiments took place 19–22 June 1969.

Nearly three years later, in April 1972, Trinity House decided that Casquets, Hanois and Alderney lighthouses should have helicopter personnel reliefs, and that their relief boatmen were to be given notice.

The installation of a helicopter service for Bishop Rock came a step nearer when, in 1973, Trinity House resolved to make provision for a helipad, at a cost of £15,000, should an experiment at Wolf Rock be successful. Here, building a helipad was underway and a six-month trial of reliefs was to start on 3 November by Bristow Helicopters Ltd.

## 100TH ANNIVERSARY CELEBRATED

The centenary of the first exhibition of light at Bishop Rock lighthouse was an event worthy of celebration. The Trinity House yacht *Patricia*, and tender *Satellite* sailed over to the Isles of Scilly for the occasion.

Special services were held at St Mary's Church on Sunday 30 August 1958. *Satellite* was opened to the public and hundreds of people were able to look around the vessel. On 1 September, the actual anniversary day, when *Satellite* was moored up in St Mary's roads, another service took place on board, to which island launches brought out about one hundred people. The service was conducted by the Right Rev J. Wellington, Assistant Bishop of Truro, Rev J. Gillett, Chaplain of the Isles of Scilly, and the Methodist Minister, Rev R. Crewes.

The yacht *Patricia* then sailed out to the lighthouse to try and land Elder Brethren for an inspection, but the wind had increased making this impossible. The Principal Keeper, A. Nethercott, was to have been presented with a table lamp made from serpentine stone so, instead, it was winched up to him in a basket. Not only did PK Nethercott receive a lamp but so too did every surviving PK who had served at Bishop Rock.

The keepers from the Wolf Rock and Round Island lighthouses and the Seven Stones lightvessel sent messages by radio to the keepers at Bishop Rock. A poem was recited to them by the Right Rev Wellington, which was reciprocated by one PK Nethercott had written for the occasion.

That evening and a couple of evenings later, Captain Prideaux of the Mission for Deep Sea Fishermen presented a film show in the church hall of life on British lighthouses and scenes of spectacular seas. Proceeds from these and from service collections went towards a television for the keepers at Wolf Rock lighthouse.

## LISTING REFUSED

The importance of Bishop Rock lighthouse had been recognised by the Ministry of Housing & Local Government. They proposed to include it and the Daymark on St Martin's (built in 1687 by Trinity House and Mr Thomas Ekins)[17] in the lists of buildings of special architectural or historic interest being compiled in 1959. But, for some reason, Trinity House did not want the lighthouse included, so just the Daymark was listed. Perhaps they feared any future alterations required to the lighthouse would prove more difficult to undertake if listed.

*A keeper at the light.* GIBSON ARCHIVE

# Chapter Thirteen

# 1974 ONWARDS

A time of major change for Bishop Rock lighthouse followed, the likes of which James Walker and the Douglass men could never have foreseen. They would have been fascinated by the installation of a helipad and the concept of automation.

In April 1974 a scheme for modernisation, initially costing £93,000, was put forward and which was to revolutionise the workings of the lighthouse. The renewal of the fog signal, the installation of a Racon (an electronic responder used to mark maritime hazards), a fire extinguishing system, a power operated winch, further improvements to the dwellings and, most important of all, the construction of a helicopter landing platform, were all recommended:

Main scheme: £70,000
Helideck: £23,000

Over a year later, and not surprisingly, the costing had to be revised to £128,000.

Trinity House approved the installation of a temporary electric fog signal at Bishop Rock in early February 1975, with a character of one blast of three seconds duration every 30 seconds. Six weeks notice was given to mariners. The temporary electric fog signal took over from the explosive fog signal on 25 June. Its character remained the same with Morse (N) 2 blasts every 90 seconds.

This temporary electric fog signal was permanently discontinued and replaced by a Supertyfon fog signal on 1 February 1977. On 8 March, a listening trial for this took place on the Trinity House Vessel (THV) *Stella* by Capt I. R. C. Saunders. Further trials were carried out on 19 May by Capt T. Woodfield. At the same time, he carried out trials on the new uncoded Radar Beacon (Racon) at Bishop Rock, which had been brought into operation on 21 April.

The helipad was designed by David Vennings, the Director of Engineering at Trinity House. Work on it began in August 1975 with the construction of a tubular scaffold platform. On 12 August, two compressors were flown from St Mary's airport to the lighthouse. Deep

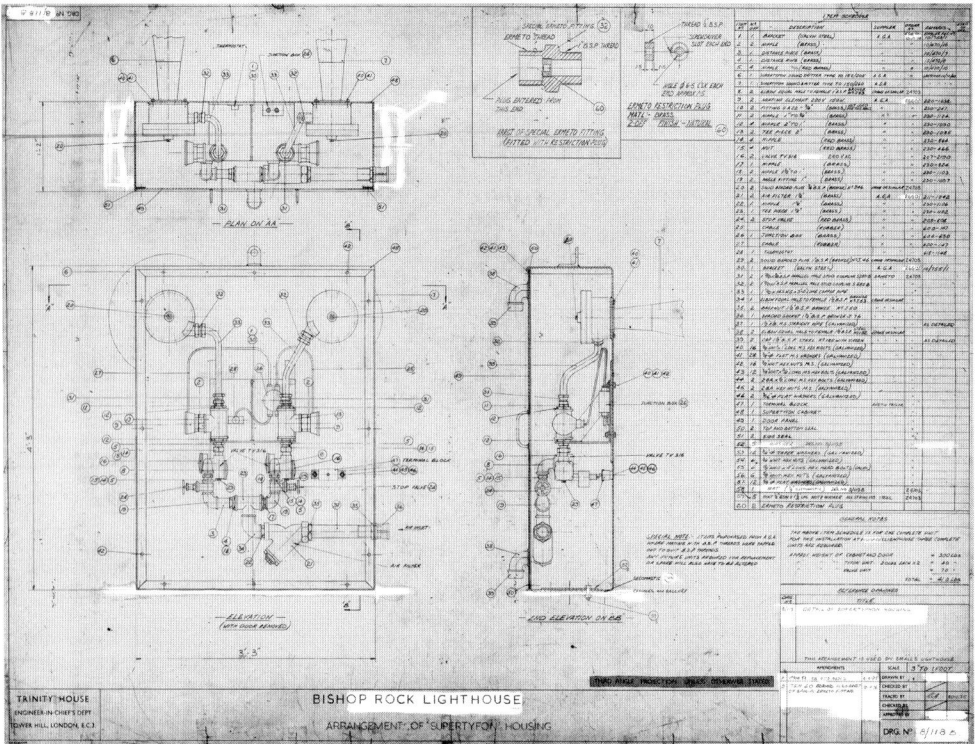

*Housing for the Supertyfon fog signal.*
TRINITY HOUSE

holes of 17 feet were drilled into the lighthouse walls for the rock anchor bolts which were to be secured with resin grout. Those drilling the holes, under the direction of Mr G. E. MacDonald-Jones, the District Inspector of Works for Trinity House, were Trinity House employees, P. Keane, B. Harvey, G. Davey, and H. Kemp.[1]

The construction of the helicopter landing platform, was undertaken by Blight & White Ltd at a cost of £22,326.61. It was finished in August 1976, and won the 1977 Structural Steel Design Award. During construction, the top tier of the lens was removed and retained at Penzance District Depot, which later became the Trinity House National Lighthouse Centre (now closed). The signpost on top of the lighthouse, with Land's End shown in one direction and USA in another, was removed also.

Having completed the helipad, the tower was re-wired by two electricians. On 27 August 1976, one of these electricians, Mr George Tindale, fell 40 feet from the landing stage into the sea while handling equipment. He was rescued by divers who were nearby, and taken to Treliske Hospital at Truro suffering from a broken ankle and other injuries.[2]

In 1975, before the nature of reliefs was to change from boat to helicopter, *Blue Peter*, the BBC children's programme, sent out one of their presenters, Lesley Judd, to be filmed both landing and being taken off the lighthouse in the traditional way. The weather was not good and, according to Mike Hicks who had taken her out there with his crew in the wooden boat *Sea King*, waves were coming over the stern. Lesley was quite upfront about how she felt:

'Bishop Rock lighthouse is one of the filming locations I'll never, ever forget. Landing on the lighthouse by breeches buoy was frightening enough, but getting off was terrifying'.[3] According to the Blue Peter website, Lesley's harness snapped, leaving her with no support had she lost her grip on the rope. Being unused to rough seas, this must have been a daunting assignment, especially with television cameras recording her every move.

Lesley paid tribute to the skills of Mike Hicks and his crew, and explained how they had to keep the rope taut at all times to prevent her from crashing against the lighthouse, and also to keep the boat in position just off the rocks.

In 1974 the length of duty on the lighthouse had changed from two to one month's duration.[4] On one relief, two men were taken off, while on the next, one man was removed. This pattern was alternated. The change had been met with approval by the keepers. As one explained to Tony

*Plan of the helipad.*
TRINITY HOUSE

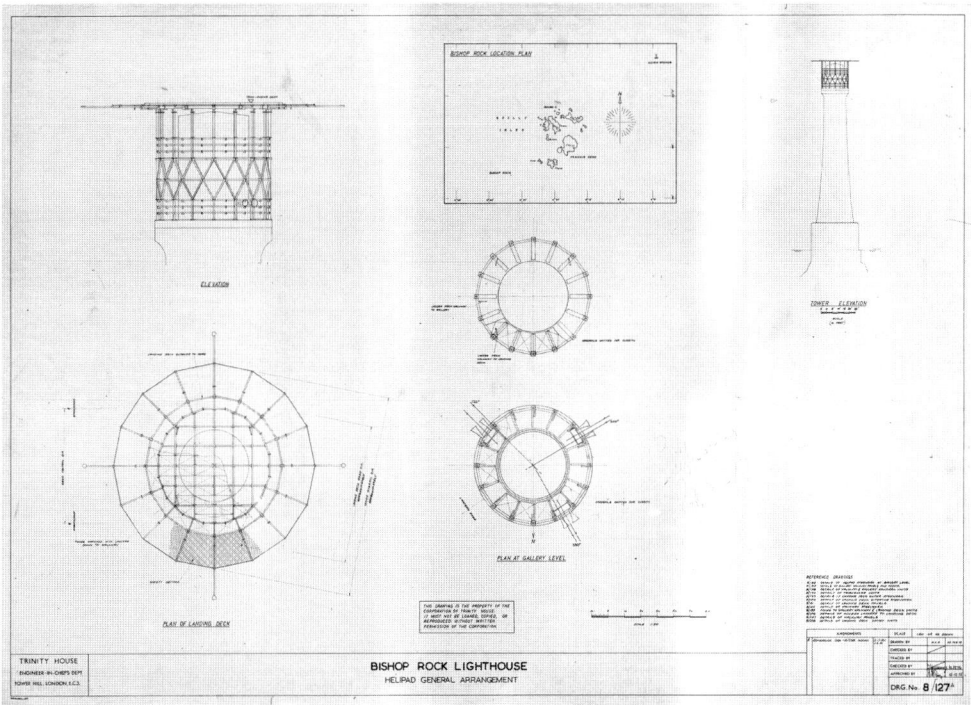

BISHOP ROCK LIGHTHOUSE
HELIPAD GENERAL ARRANGEMENT

Parker, two months was too long; 'you'll get more of a variety in keepers … then the air, it'll be fresher, there'll be more life in it to breathe. You won't get men going ashore pasty-faced in colour and pasty-faced inside. They'll be more human both ways round, when they're off on the light and when they're ashore'.[5]

In July 1976 the last Bishop Rock boat relief took place. This was a truly significant occasion in the history of the lighthouse, ending an era of

*The helipad.*
ELISABETH
STANBROOK

118 years. From now on, technology would take over with air travel becoming the main mode of transport. Winched down into the waiting *Lily of Laguna* were PK Handel 'Andy' Bluer, and AKs Russell Pape and Richard Kinver, greeted by George and Mike Hicks who had undertaken the reliefs for nearly twenty-five years. The whole episode was watched by pleasure boats full of spectators and television teams. The relief of the lighthouse keepers had become a tourist attraction during the summer months, and it was now at an end.

The first relief by helicopter took place on 10 August 1976 with the changeover of three keepers. The operation took three hours longer than usual because the event was being filmed for Blue Peter, and the keepers had to keep re-enacting the relief for the benefit of the cameras! All reliefs were now between St Mary's airport and the lighthouse; a trip of just ten minutes. Supplies such as water were also delivered by helicopter. The only delay in the relief would be because of fog as a helicopter could fly in up to a Gale Force 10.

The helicopters initially used for the reliefs were two Bolkow BO 105D twin-engined helicopters on contract from Management Aviation Ltd of Bourn, Cambridge. They were also used to transport the Engineer-in-Chief's personnel to and from the lighthouse with the equipment and materials. An underslung cargo hook was fitted for this purpose. They were manufactured by Messerschmitt Bolkow-Blohn (M.B.B.) in Munich, West Germany. They had two Allison 250-C20 gas turbine engines.

In 1979, Bond Helicopters (formerly Management Aviation Ltd) were given the contract to fly for Trinity House. Their work included the reliefs for Bishop Rock and Round Island lighthouses.

*The first relief by helicopter.* GIBSON ARCHIVE

INSIDE THE LIGHTHOUSE

An interesting description of the interior of the lighthouse in 1981 is given by PK Harold Taylor, and complements the others given above: Steep iron ladders with rope handrails led to the lower part of the tower. The base floor contained the water storage tanks, the engine oil, a deep freeze and a rope locker (which had once been a lavatory). The first floor was the main fuel oil storage area with large tanks placed around the walls and one in the middle. There was also an electric fuel distribution pump.

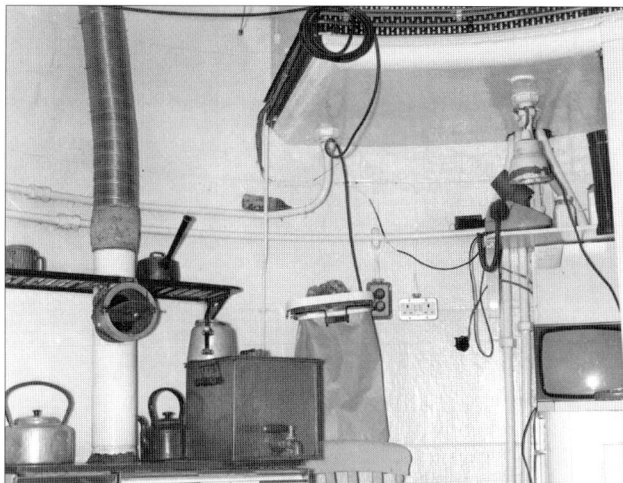

*The kitchen in 1975.*
TRINITY HOUSE

The second floor was the lower engine room and workshop, with two generators. Mr Taylor described how the window had been made to keep the sea out but allow the cooling air in. He recalled how unbearably hot and noisy the room was when in operation.

The third floor housed three oil tanks 'which gravity fed to the engine room below'. Rubbish was also collected here, and there was a gas-powered shower and an Elsan bucket. On the fourth floor was the kitchen. This was smaller than the rooms below, with a gas cooker, a table in the middle and fixed benches around it. The food storage cupboards were fixed above head height over a bench, 'and the only way to get at the shelves was to stand on the table'.

The bedroom was on the fifth floor with its banana-shaped beds and storage cupboards. There was also an electric storage heater.

On the sixth floor was the sitting room. Mr Taylor thought this was once the original kitchen as it used to have a fireplace or range. The weight tube also used to go down through the centre of the room, but as the lens was now driven by electric motors, this had been removed. There was another storage heater in this room, three radio transmitters and a

*The lighthouse bedroom with the banana-shaped bunks.*
TRINITY HOUSE

television. Shelves were lined with books and there were more food cupboards. There was also a shipping band transmitter and a new apparatus for VHF communication, together with another set for communicating with the helicopter.

The service room was on the seventh floor, with two radio transmitter engines, and two compressed air engines for the fog signal suspended from the ceiling. There were engines that did not work too. These were supposed to provide daylight power for the lighthouse. Apparently, no mechanic could ever get them into working order during Mr Taylor's service.

The floor above housed the original lens, 'a monstrous construction'. There were two lenses up here because it had been intended from the wick lamp days 'that in clear visibility one lens was lit, but in poor visibility both would be used. In electrification they had utilised this to the effect that the main light was exhibited low down, and in the event of a power failure, the battery light would illuminate the top lens.'[6] There was also a 'toilet bucket' which was emptied from this room into the 'passing wind'.

The fuel delivery had been undertaken by a Trinity House ship, but this changed during Mr Taylor's time to relief by helicopter.

AUTOMATION AND THE END OF AN ERA

On 21 December 1992, after months of work, the lighthouse became automated, and it is now operated from Trinity House Harwich Operations Control Centre. Just one keeper stayed on the lighthouse during this time, and shared the accommodation with the workmen. When the keeper was off duty, one of the workmen would take over the watch.

The automation work, carried out by East Cowes Automation Team, included more or less gutting the structure and then installing new batteries, engines and wiring, some of which were delivered by boat. For example, on 4 May 1992, pyrotechnics were delivered by *Black Swan*, and removed the time-expired ones; drills were delivered on 13 June; the automation gear was landed on 7 July; *Sea King* landed electrical items on 28 July; more engine parts were delivered by *Black Swan* on 16 August; and 6 ½ tons of batteries were landed on 25 August. Other deliveries such as stores and water took place throughout by helicopter.[7]

To automate the lighthouse, the top element of the optic was removed so that an emergency light could be fitted. This would only be used if both of the main lamps failed, the optic rotation failed, or the power supply failed to either of these. A battery would provide at least 35 hours of power. The Racon had its own battery for its power supply. The optic is still a hyper-radial rotating asymmetrical dioptric lens (1,330mm focal length), with ten panels, but it is no longer biform. Two 400 watt MBI lamps replaced the 240v 1500 watt filament lamps, and the minimum range of light became 24 nautical miles.

The Supertyfon fog signal by now had been replaced with an electric signal which was operated by a fog detector, but the signal character of Morse (N) every 90 seconds remained. The fog signal was discontinued altogether in 13 July 2007.

Power became generated by replacement engine sets. A solar system, used in some other lighthouses, was considered to be inadequate for the amount of power needed. A 'cycle charge system', which is a periodic running of the diesel alternator when the battery charge falls, was installed to help reduce the consumption and cost of fuel needed to continuously run the engines. Maintenance visits now would be every six months, and the fuel capacity had been enlarged so that at least 18 months worth of fuel instead of six could be held there. Bed spaces for five maintenance staff were installed plus provision for a water capacity of fifty man days. A microwave link and aeronautical and marine VHF channels now provided the means of communication.

Former Bishop Rock SAK Gordon Partridge described going out to the lighthouse for maintenance duties once it was unmanned: 'We would be out there for several nights at a time in order to effect our task list. I have to say that, having served at Bishop when fully manned, then to return with only the silicon chip manning it, it was eerie! No aroma of hot coffee on the edge of the Rayburn (indeed, no Rayburn either!), no warm welcome from fellow keepers already on the station. As I have said many times before, the lighthouse towers were the bodies and the keepers their souls; once the keepers had been withdrawn, all that remained were buildings, functioning well, yes, but, breathing on their own, no!'

The lightning conductor, which had run down the inside of the lighthouse, was replaced by three external runs, each with its own earth rod. 'Two orbital rings have been positioned at suitable points in the tower and connected to the vertical run. The station earthing system utilises the final earth termination of the lightning system but is run separately within the tower'.[8] Fire detection, dehumidification and heating facilities were also fitted.

Automating Bishop Rock lighthouse cost Trinity House £450,000. It was estimated at the time that the cost of operating it without keepers would fall from £191,000 per annum to £96,000. Over the following fifteen years, it was estimated that a saving of £975,000 would be made.[9]

With this automation came the end of a 134-year-old era. No longer were lighthouse keepers required to keep the lamp flashing every night, or the fog signal sounding in thick weather. The last keeper, AK Peter Robson, was airlifted to St Just and was later posted to the Needles lighthouse. He signed off his last watch, at 0630 hours, to Mr Taylor, one

*Peter Robson, the last keeper to leave Bishop Rock lighthouse.*
ALK PHOTO NO. N626

*The last ever entry in the Bishop Rock Lighthouse Journal on 21 December 1992. ALK B582*

of the automation team. These were the last names recorded in the Lighthouse Journal.

The keepers' houses were no longer required, and they were sold to a housing association.

Sea and weather continue to affect the tower. In January 1990, the power of the waves made the tower shudder so much that in the amenity room, some fluorescent tubes and broom handles came tumbling off the fuel tanks where they were being stored. The entrance door was also badly damaged.[10]

On 3 February 1994 the doors into Bishop Rock lighthouse suffered major damage. Two short articles in *Lamp*, published in 2002, described how a storm from the south, of about 80 knots, hit the Isles of Scilly, and the sea behaved accordingly. It was during this storm that the doors were battered, with one being wrenched off its hinges. The doors had a design loading of three tons per square foot, were cast in bronze and weighed over 2cwt / 100 kg each, so achieving the damage was no mean feat. The missing door was found, by Trinity House staff arriving on 5 February, 'embedded in the shower cabinet in the base of the tower having demolished a sturdy mahogany door on its way'.[11] The doors had to be removed and replaced quickly, and a temporary barrier of steel plates were installed while new ones were being made.

But what caused this damage? The sea alone, powerful as she is, could never have achieved this on her own. There have been various theories put forward,[12] but all have been inconclusive. Reports of items of lost cargo in the area were made, such as baulks of teak and floating containers, which could have been carried 40 feet up by the sea to crash into the door. This appears to be the most likely explanation.

On 25 December 2001 Bishop Rock lighthouse was leased to the Duchy of Cornwall for 20 years until 2021 at £150 p.a.[13]

The current maintenance schedule comprises 3-monthly husbandry inspections by the local attendant, as well as annual inspections by Trinity House technicians, when the diesel engines are maintained to standard. Maintenance work is undertaken as needed. A recent photograph by Joy Adcock, which appears in Christopher Nicholson's fine book, *Rock Lighthouses of Britain* (2006 edition), shows the outer granite walls of the lighthouse starting to suffer the effects of constant pounding by the sea, causing the massive stone blocks to become pitted. In July 2007, three workmen carrying out repairs to the helipad ran out of milk. They were able to acquire a delivery of, not only milk, but fruit and newspapers too, via the lifeboat out on exercise.[14]

With global warming being in the forefront of people's minds at present, Bishop Rock lighthouse will most likely play a part in Trinity House's ongoing reduction of its 'carbon footprint'. This will involve reducing the use of the diesel engines, and supplementing them with alternative energy sources.[15]

## LANDMARK FOR RACES

Not only is Bishop Rock lighthouse an important landmark for mariners, but for transatlantic events too including the Blue Riband. This is an award presented to ship owners who set a record for the fastest sailing time between Bishop Rock lighthouse and New York's Ambrose light-tower. The Blue Riband was begun in the 1860s as a means of shipowners displaying the speed of their vessels. The winners flew a blue pennant from the topmast of the ship and then, in 1935, a trophy was introduced by Sir Harold Hale, owner of the shipping company, Hale Brothers. The Hale Trophy is now awarded to each winner.

In August 1936 the 3,400-mile race was won by the British liner *Queen Mary*, and took three days, 23 hours and 53 minutes to complete while, in July 1952, the race was won by *S.S. United States* which took three days, ten hours and 40 minutes. This ship held the record for many years. More recently, in June 1986, Richard Branson broke this record in his *Virgin Atlantic II* with three days, eight hours and 31 minutes. However, the trustees of the award were reluctant to give him the trophy because his boat was not of a commercial type, and he had stopped to refuel during the voyage. Nevertheless, it was a beaten record, but on 25

*Destreiro passing Bishop Rock lighthouse.*
GIBSON ARCHIVE

July 1989, this was broken by Tom Gentry, an American, in his boat *Gentry Eagle*, which took two days, 14 hours and seven minutes. To commemorate the occasion, Richard Branson had a three foot silver model of Bishop Rock lighthouse made to present to him.

In 1990 the British Hoverspeed *Great Britain*, a catamaran, broke the *S.S. United States* record, taking three days, seven hours and 54 minutes, and was awarded the Blue Riband and trophy. Eight years later, this accolade passed to Scandlines *Cat-Link V* which took two days, 20 hours and nine minutes. In 1992 *Destreiro* managed the crossing in 58 hours, 34 minutes and five seconds, but as she was a privately owned yacht, she was also denied the award. The record will continue to be broken.

The lighthouse is fondly regarded by Americans and British alike when travelling eastwards across the expansive Atlantic Ocean. One American told the author that, as a boy (1940s/50s) he could remember being on a passenger liner en route for Britain. He suddenly heard an excited hubbub coming from the deck, so he went up to see what was happening. Bishop Rock lighthouse had just been seen on the horizon and people were gathering to watch the tower rising up from the sea like an old friend. It was an emotional occasion, forever in his memory.

*A St Mary's Boatmen Association ticket for the Bishop Rock lighthouse trip.*
ELISABETH STANBROOK

Bishop Rock lighthouse on the Isles of Scilly remains one of the country's most famous lighthouses, with many visitor boat trips taking place from the inhabited islands to see this famous structure. It is also used in

162

the logos of both the Council of the Isles of Scilly and the Area of Outstanding Natural Beauty (AONB). The Radio Scilly logo is also of a lighthouse.

Very few small, isolated rocks can boast a documented history stretching back to at least 1302, but Bishop Rock possesses this accolade. Through the ages it has witnessed death by judicial execution and the tragic drowning of hapless mariners through endless shipwrecks. But, from the mid-nineteenth century, it has played a major role in saving lives through the remarkable feat of engineering overseen by some of the most eminent Victorian engineers of the time, notably the three Douglass men and James Walker. Through the auspices of Trinity House Corporation, they were able to provide an essential lifeline to sailors and mariners from all over the world who found themselves in these treacherous waters and, today, despite major technological upheavals and innovations in both sailing and lighthouse management, it is still as vital as ever. From land, it is the lighthouse that is foremost in peoples' minds as they gaze out across the Western Rocks towards its silhouette, a building which stands tall at the westernmost boundary of southern England.

In the words of William Tregarthen Douglass:

There are few if any lighthouses of more importance to sailors, or of more professional interest to the engineer, than the Bishop Rock.[16]

## BISHOP ROCK LIGHTHOUSE SPECIFICATIONS TODAY

Height of Tower: 49 metres
Height of Light above MHW: 44 metres
Light Source: 400 watt MBI lamp
Optic: Hyper-radial 1,330mm rotating
Character: Two white group flashes every 15 seconds
Candle Power: 2,600,000 candela
Range of Light: 24 nautical miles
Fog Warning Apparatus: Morse (N) every 90 seconds

CRO Cornwall Record Office
GLL Guildhall Library, London
TNA The National Archives, Kew

Notes to Introduction

1. North, I. W. *A Week in the Isles of Scilly* E. Rowe, Penzance 1850 p.44
2. Sobel, Dava *Longitude* Fourth Estate, London 1996
3. Padel, O. J. *Cornish Place-Names* Alison Hodge 1988 p.53
4. Larn, Richard *Cornish Shipwrecks: The Isles of Scilly* David & Charles 1971 p.33
5. Thomas, Charles *Exploration of a Drowned Landscape* B. T. Batsford Ltd, London 1985 p.149
6. Padel, O. J. *Cornish Place-Names* Alison Hodge 1988 pp.53-4
7. Whetter, James *Cornwall in the 13th Century* 1998 p.29
8. TNA JUST/1/118 m.53 verso Hundred of Penwith 1302
9. TNA JUST 1/112
10. GLL MS 30004, Vol 7 & Greeves, Tom 'Who Built the Daymark on St Martin's and Why?' in *The Scillonian* Winter 2007/8 pp.164-7
11. www.trinityhouse.co.uk
12. www.trinityhouse.co.uk

Notes to Chapter One: 1839 to 1846

1. *Minutes of the Proceedings of The Institution of Civil Engineers Vol CVIII* 1891-92 Part II p.207
2. Larn, Richard *Cornish Shipwrecks: The Isles of Scilly* David & Charles 1971 p.44

Notes to Chapter Two: 1847 to February 1850

1. GLL MS 30052 Vol 6
2. Llewellyn, Sam *Emperor Smith The Man Who Built Scilly* The Dovecote Press 2005 p.51
3. GLL MS 30010 Vol 35
4. *Minutes of the Proceedings of The Institution of Civil Engineers Vol CVIII* 1891-92 p.209
5. www.trinityhouse.co.uk
6. GLL MS 30004 Vol 24
7. GLL MS 30010 Vol 36
8. www.divernet.com

9. *Minutes of the Proceedings of The Institution of Civil Engineers Vol CVIII* 1891-92 p.210

10. *Minutes of the Proceedings of The Institution of Civil Engineers Vol CVIII* 1891-92 p.230

NOTES TO CHAPTER THREE: 1850 TO 1858

1. GLL MS 30004 Vol 24

2. GLL MS 30052 Vol 6

3. GLL MS 30052 Vol 6

4. GLL MS 30052 Vol 6

5. Pers. comm. with David Hooley, 26.6.2006

6. Cornwall Sites & Monument Record PRN 7066

7. Grigson, Geoffrey *The Scilly Isles* Gerald Duckworth & Co Ltd 1977 (reprinted from 1948) p.52

8. Pers. comm. with Colin Sturmer, October 2005

9. Aldridge, Wendy *Hobnails and Seaboots* George G. Harrap & Co Ltd 1957 (reprint) p.221

10. GLL MS 30004 Vol 24

11. GLL MS 30010 Vol 37

12. Jackson, Derrick *Lighthouses of England & Wales* David & Charles 1975; Mudd, David *Cornwall & Scilly Peculiar* Bossiney Books 1979 & www.trinityhouse.co.uk

13. Tarrant, Michael *Trinity House The Super Silent Service* Gomer Press 1998 p.56

14. GLL MS 30052 Vol 7

15. GLL MS 30010 Vol 37

16. Williams, Thomas *Life of Sir James Nicholas Douglass FRS* Longmans Green & Co 1900 p.18

17. Hague, Douglas B. *Lighthouses of Wales Their Architecture and Archaeology* Royal Commission on the Ancient and Historical Monuments of Wales 1994 p.130 & Douglass, William Tregarthen *The New Eddystone Lighthouse* The Institution of Civil Engineers 1883 p.22

18. Williams, Thomas *Life of Sir James Nicholas Douglass FRS* Longmans Green & Co 1900 p.18

19. *Minutes of the Proceedings of The Institution of Civil Engineers Vol CVIII* 1891-92 Part II p.238

20. *Minutes of the Proceedings of The Institution of Civil Engineers Vol CVIII* 1891-92 Part II p.229

21. Williams, Thomas *Life of Sir James Nicholas Douglass FRS* Longmans Green & Co 1900 p.15

22. Williams, Thomas *Life of Sir James Nicholas Douglass FRS* Longmans Green & Co 1900 p.15

23. Williams, Thomas *Life of Sir James Nicholas Douglass FRS* Longmans Green & Co 1900 p.23

24. GLL MS 30025 Vol 21

25. Williams, *Thomas Life of Sir James Nicholas Douglass FRS* Longmans Green & Co 1900 p.14

26. GLL MS 30010 Vol 38

27. *Minutes of the Proceedings of The Institution of Civil Engineers Vol XV* 1855 p.8

28. TNA WO 44/572

29. GLL MS 30052 Vol 7

30. GLL MS 30052 Vol 7

31. Maybee, Robert *The Scillonian Poet* Isle of Scilly Museum Publication No.9 1973 p.12

32. Maybee, Robert *The Scillonian Poet* Isle of Scilly Museum Publication No.9 1973 p.19-20

33. GLL MS 30052 Vol 7

34. GLL MS 30010 Vol 41

35. GLL MS 30108 Vol 5

36. GLL MS 30108 Vol 5

37. GLL MS30010 Vol 41

38. GLL MS 30025 Vol 24

39. GLL MS 30010 Vol.41

40. GLL MS 30052 Vol.7

41. GLL MS 30010 Vol 41

42. GLL MS 30004 Vol 27

43. Noall, Cyril *Cornish Lights and Shipwrecks* D. Bradford Barton Ltd 1968 p.28

44. TNA MT 9/6

45. TNA MT 9/6

46. Stanier, Peter *South West Granite – A History of the Granite Industry in Cornwall & Devon* Cornish Hillside Publications 1999 p.202

47. GLL MS 30025 Vol 26

48. GLL MS 30025 Vol 26

NOTES TO CHAPTER FOUR: 1859 TO 1873

1. Report of the Commissioners appointed to enquire into the Condition and Management of Lights, Buoys, and Beacons 1861 Vols I & II. (Vol XXV 2793)

2. GLL MS 30025 Vol 26

3. GLL MS 30052 Vol 8

4. Report of the Commissioners appointed to enquire into the Condition and Management of Lights, Buoys, and Beacons 1861 Vols I & II. (Vol XXV 2793) p.13 & Esquiros, Alphonse *Cornwall and its Coast* Chapman & Hall 1856 p.279

5. GLL MS 30010 Vol 42
6. *Minutes of the Proceedings of The Institution of Civil Engineers Vol CVIII* 1891-92 Part II p.211
7. GLL MS 30052 Vol 8
8. www.divernet.com
9. GLL MS 30052 Vol 9
10. Boyle, Martin *Bishop Rock Lighthouse* B. & T. Publications 1997 p.16
11. GLL MS 30025 Vol 31
12. GLL MS 30025 Vol 33
13. GLL MS30025 Vol 34
14. GLL MS 30052 Vol 9

NOTES TO CHAPTER FIVE: 1874 TO 1881
1. *The Cornish Telegraph* 22.4.1874 p.4
2. GLL MS 30010 Vol 50
3. *Minutes of the Proceedings of The Institution of Civil Engineers Vol. CVIII* 1891-92 Part II p.211
4. CRO Court Record Book Scilly 1835-1917 10.5.1875
5. GLL MS 30010 Vol 50
6. GLL MS 30010 Vol 52
7. GLL MS 30025 Vol 44

NOTES TO CHAPTER SIX: 1882 TO 1888
1. *South Devon & South Cornwall* Dulan & Co. 1885 p.148
2. Stanier, Peter *South West Granite – A History of the Granite Industry in Cornwall & Devon* Cornish Hillside Publications 1999 p.9
3. Stanier, Peter *South West Granite – A History of the Granite Industry in Cornwall & Devon* Cornish Hillside Publications 1999 p.115
4. Extracts from Order Book Bishop Rock ALK No. P468
5. K. Trethewey *How Lighthouses Work* obsolete website nd
6. *Minutes of the Proceedings of The Institution of Civil Engineers Vol CVIII* 1891-92 Part II p.218
7. Extracts from Order Book Bishop Rock ALK No. P468
8. *Minutes of the Proceedings of The Institution of Civil Engineers Vol CVIII* 1891-92 Part II p.220
9. Pers comm between Norman Christopher & Tom Greeves 21.2.2007
10. *Minutes of the Proceedings of The Institution of Civil Engineers Vol CVIII* 1891-92 Part II p.220
11. Pers comm with Joan Tabar 13.5.05
12. Taylor, Harold *A Light at the Top* CD nd p.210

NOTES TO CHAPTER SEVEN: 1889 TO 1899
1. GLL MS 30010 Vol 61

NOTES TO CHAPTER EIGHT: 1900 TO 1913

1. Extracts from Order Book Bishop Rock ALK No. P468
2. Lewis, W. J. *Ceaseless Vigil: My lonely years in the lighthouse service* George Harrap & Co Ltd 1970 p.13
3. Jenkins, A. J. *Gigs and Cutters of the Isles of Scilly* Maggie Tucker (reprint) 2002 (book unpaginated)
4. *The Scillonian* Winter 1975-6 p.106

NOTES TO CHAPTER NINE: THE GREAT WAR YEARS

1. Bowley, R. L. *Scilly at War* Bowley Publications Ltd 2001 p.169
2. Extracts from Order Book Bishop Rock ALK No. P468
3. Gordon Medlicott 'Put That Light Out – Trinity House at War' *Lamp* 76 May 2008 p.17

NOTES TO CHAPTER TEN: THE INTER-WAR YEARS

1. Lewis, W. J. *Ceaseless Vigil: My lonely years in the lighthouse service* George Harrap & Co Ltd 1970 pp.12-13
2. Extracts from Order Book Scilly Dwellings ALK No. P468
3. Gumbrell, Patricia *Last of the Line* Whittles Publishing 2005 p.41
4. Pers comm with Patricia Gumbrell 1.5.2007
5. Gumbrell, Patricia *Last of the Line* Whittles Publishing 2005 p.44
6. Lewis, W. J. *Ceaseless Vigil: My lonely years in the lighthouse service* George Harrap & Co Ltd 1970 pp.27-8
7. Lighthouse Keepers File, Isles of Scilly Museum
8. The author is indebted to Gerry Douglas-Sherwood for this information
9. Lewis, W. J. *Ceaseless Vigil: My lonely years in the lighthouse service* George Harrap & Co Ltd 1970 p.10
10. Lewis, W. J. *Ceaseless Vigil: My lonely years in the lighthouse service* George Harrap & Co Ltd 1970 p.10-11

NOTES TO CHAPTER ELEVEN: SECOND WORLD WAR

1. *The Scillonian* 1953
2. GLL MS 30076 Vol 1

NOTES TO CHAPTER TWELVE: 1946 TO 1973

1. *Lamp* 56 September 2002 p.19
2. GLL MS 30010 Vol 113
3. *Picture Post* 1 February 1947 p.31
4. *The Scillonian* Easter 1947 p.33
5. GLL MS 30010 Vol 133
6. Douglas-Sherwood, Gerry *A Glossary of Lighthouse Service Terminology* Association of Lighthouse Keepers 2000
7. Tarrant, Michael *Trinity House – The Super Silent Service* Gomer Press 1998 p.58

8. Tarrant, Michael *Trinity House – The Super Silent Service* Gomer Press 1998 p.58

9. *The Scillonian* March 1948 p.43

10. Woodman, R. & Wilson, J. *The Lighthouses of Trinity House* Thomas Reed Publications 2002 p.75

11. *The Scillonian* Winter 2007/8 p.178

12. *The Scillonian* Winter 1969/70 p.215

13. Parker, Tony *Lighthouse* Eland Publishing Ltd 2006 pp.168-9

14. Parker, Tony *Lighthouse* Eland Publishing Ltd 2006 pp.169-70

15. Watts, Jeremy Reseigh *Scilly Through the Eyes of The 'Duchess of Auriga'* Shepeard-Walwyn (Publishers) Ltd 2005 p.161

16. Parker, Tony *Lighthouse* Eland Publishing Ltd 2006 pp.221-2

17. GLL MS 30025 Vol 122

NOTES TO CHAPTER THIRTEEN: 1974 ONWARDS

1. *The Scillonian* Winter 1975/6 p.19

2. *The Scillonian* Winter 1976/77 pp.39-40

3. www.bbc.co.uk/cult BBC

4. *The Scillonian* Winter 1976/77 p.10

5. Parker, Tony *Lighthouse* Eland Publishing Ltd 2006 p.283

6. Taylor, Harold *A Light at the Top* CD nd p.212

7. *Bishop Rock Lighthouse Journal* From 1 May 1992

8. *Flash* Trinity House 1993 p.8

9. *Flash* Trinity House 1993 p.7

10. *The Guardian* March 31 1990

11. *Lamp* 57 December 2002 p.16

12. *Lamp* 57 December 2002 pp.15-16

13. Duchy of Cornwall office (Isles of Scilly)

14. *The Scillonian* Winter 2007/8 p.88

15. Pers comm with Neil Jones, Trinity House, 12 March 2007

16. *Minutes of the Proceedings of The Institution of Civil Engineers Vol CVIII* 1891-92 Part II p.207

# BISHOP ROCK
## LIGHTHOUSE KEEPERS

PK – Principal Keeper
AK – Assistant Keeper
SAK – Supernumerary Assistant
    Keeper

This list is incomplete in terms of both dates and names, as no complete record exists. Where the status of the keeper is unknown, it is left blank.

1858-62: John H. Watson PK
1858: Thomas Hallam AK
1858-1862: Henry Williams AK
1858-1866: John Williams AK & PK
1860s: Thomas Arnold AK
1861: William Lightfoot
1866-8: George William Brown AK
1869-74: Joseph Upton AK
1863-69: Francis Ellis AK
1870-1: J. Sibert AK
1871: Samuel Rambridge AK
1871: Mr Cock AK
1875-7: W. J. Batton
1875: Samuel Rogers
1875: George Ray Gould AK
1875: William Mortimer AK
1875: James Daniel AK
1877: Thomas J. Nicholson AK
1877-81: J. Lloyd
1877-9: R. E. Elliston
1877-9: J. T. Woodruff
1877-9: W. C. Lewis
1877: E. Hilder, PK
1877: William Joseph Batton
1879-85: John Robert Hall AK
1879-85: James Thomas AK

1880-4: Francis James Evans AK
1881: Mr James Lloyd PK
1881-7: John William Troth AK
1884-9: J. Mitchell
1885-91: George H. Dunsford AK
1885-91: Martin Pender AK
1887-90: J. J. Saunders
1889-92: George Smith
1889: Samuel Rogers
1891-4: A. Dale
1891-2: William H. Trehair SAK
1891-4: Walter Davies SAK
1891-4: W. H. Fenn
1891-4: Henry Nicholas PK
1891-4: E. A. Blackburn
1892: A. J. Boulton
1892: Mr Nicholls
1892: Mr Brown
1892-3: W. Kaye
1892-7: R. Wilson
c.1893: John W. Hall SAK
1894: Samuel R. Rambridge AK? Died
    in office
1894: J. J. Smith
c.1890s: Tom Lawrence
c.1890s: Ernest Lawrence
1894: W. Jones PK
1894-7: E. Horne
1894-7: A. E. Norton
1894-7: J. J. Sibert
1897-1901: Arthur Ernest Cook AK
1897-8: A. G. Grigg
1897-9: T. J. Nicholas
1897-9: A. S. Jackson

1898: John Ball PK - drowned in office

1898-1900: E. W. Hibbens

1898-1900: T. E. Roberts

1899-1900: E. Gould

1899-1901: S. W. Cotter

1899-1902: W. J. Kaye

1900: W. R. Rowe

1900-2: W. Bickford

1900-3: H. H. Sully

1900: E. Gould PK

1901: Ernest J. Upton

1903: Mr McBride AK

1903: Sidney R. Hicks AK drowned in office.

1903: J. B. Paskell SAK & AK

1904: W. G. Lewis PK

1905: Mr Thompson AK

1905-c.1910: Mr Watson AK & PK

1905-c.1909: Mr Parsons PK

1907: Mr Hills AK

1908: W. Jordain AK(?)

1908: J. A. Odgers AK

1911: R. J. Rashley AK(?)

1911: John Horace Hicks AK

1913: R. J. Comber PK

1913: Cuthert John Perry

1913-1918: Reginald Hartley

1916?-1920: L. H. Mitchell AK

1916: A. Blair AK

c.1916: Ernest Lawrence

c.1916: Tom Lawrence

1919: Mr Warder AK

c.1919: H. E. Howgego PK

1920: R. D. Glendener AK

1920: W. J. Slater AK

1920-1925: W. J. Lewis AK

1921: Mr Kaye PK

1921-2: J. Owens AK - resigned

c.1922: Jack Hicks AK(?)

1922: W. J. Williams AK

1922, 1923 & 1926: Harold O. Hall, SAK

1923: Mr Bowling AK & PK

1923: Mr Richards AK

1924: Thomas Charles William Abell AK

1925: Leonard Charles Hicks AK

1927: T. H. Smith, AK

1927: Henry Charles Thomas Horsley AK(?)

1928: Richard Trotter AK

c.1928: F. Roach PK

1930s: George Smith PK

1933: W. Jane, AK

1934: A. J. Norton, AK

1935-6: Frederick James Burgess AK

1936-42: F. B. Lock AK

1937-42: J. H. Curnow

1938: John Leslie Phillips AK

1939: Alfred John Minter AK

1939: C. K. Trezise AK

1940-41: D. Jones PK

1941-42: W. H. Senior PK

1942-45: A. Blair PK

1942-43: C. Price AK

1942-45: A. G. Jeffers AK

1943-44: L. O. Williams AK

1943: M. E. Richards AK

1944: Jack F. Beale AK

1945-46: J. R. Phillips AK

1945-48: A. R. P. Thomas AK

1945-47: J. H. Stanford PK

1946-48: Richard Duff AK

1947-48: J. C. W. Abell acting PK, then AK

1947: P. B. Daly

1948: M. J. Clifford AK

1948: Victor Brading

1948: D. Gregson AK

1948-51: B. S. Rattey AK

1948-50: J. C. T. Bevans AK

1948: C. J. Trezise PK

1948: W. G. Blake PK

1948: E. V. Roach PK

1948: J. Beale AK

1948: R. J. Duff AK

1948-50: E. E. Day PK

1949-51: P. Thorpe AK

1950-53: J. L. C. Burrage AK

1950-53: T. E. Doweatt PK

1951: K. J. W. Bareham AK

1951-52: W. J. Jarvis AK

1951-52: A. W. Pay AK

1952: P. Drummond AK

1952-53: C. W. Pickering AK

1952-53: D. Rands AK

1953: T. P. Hulme AK

1953: J. L. Prudence AK

1953-55: Charles H. Cherrett PK

1953: D. Rands AK

1953: T. H. Williams AK

1953: E. C. Nicholls AK

1953-54: W. E. J. Ellis AK

1953-53: R. A. Hill AK

1954-55 E. R. Lifely AK

1954: P. W. Perrel(?) AK

1954-55: T. A. Clark AK

1955: B. W. Long AK

1955: J. C. McCafferty AK

1955: B. N. Salter AK

1955: G. W. Edwards AK

1955: H. H. Allen AK

1955: V. A. Tryatt AK

1955: A. C. Nethercott PK

1963: George Peacock

1968: Russ Pape AK

1968: D. Berriman SAK

1968: F. M. Biddle PK

c.1960s?: Albert George Jeffers

1969: S. Reynolds PK

1969: D. B. W. (Dave) Spurgeon

1974: Larry Walker AK(?)

1974-1976: J. Terence Johns PK

1974-1976: Brian Stock AK

1974: D. C. Robins AK(?)

1974: C. R. Lewis AK(?)

c.1974: Dave Price AK

1976: G. Phillips AK

1976-c.1986: Tony Elvers AK

1976-1978: Russell Pape AK

1976: Handel (Andy) Bluer PK

1976: R. Kinver AK

1976 (Dec)-1977 (Jan): Gordon
   Partridge SAK

1978: Peter Halil AK

c.1978: A. R. (Alan) Libby AK

1978: Paul Michelmore AK

1978-1981: Brian Harris PK(?)

1978-1981: David Knight PK(?)

1980: Mr J. Shippey AK

1981-82: Harold Taylor PK

1981-85: Tristan Sturley AK

1981: Davy Jones AK

1981: Mr Vise AK

1985: E. J. (Ted) Dobbin PK

c.1986-1992: Colin Jones AK

1989: Dermot Cronin PK

1989-1992: Bill Arnold PK

1990: Avery Aish AK

1992: Peter Robson AK

1992: Julian van der Schuit AK

? Eddie Matthews

# ACKNOWLEDGEMENTS

I am greatly indebted to all those people who so willingly gave their help and encouragement to me during my research. Their own interest in the lighthouse was an inspiration for which I am very grateful. I would like to thank: Keith Austin, Stan and Margret Butcher (Lighthouse Duo), Ruth Chamberlain, Patricia Gumbrell, Steve Hartgroves, Graham Haslam, Alec Hicks, Mike Hicks, Dave Hooley, Ken & Teresa Howe & Sinbad, Christopher Nicholson, Gordon Partridge, Elizabeth and Paul Rutledge, Colin Sturmer, Joan Taber, Harold Taylor, Tony Thomas and Peggy Upham.

I am also very grateful to the following associations, libraries, museums and record offices for their invaluable help: Association of Lighthouse Keepers; British Library; Cornish Studies Library, Redruth; Cornwall Record Office, Truro; Guildhall Library, London; Institution of Civil Engineers; Amanda Martin, Curator Isles of Scilly Museum; The National Archive; National Monuments Register; Ordnance Survey; Plymouth & West Devon Record Office; Mary L. Robertson, Chief Curator of Manuscript, Huntington Library, USA; Royal Cornwall Museum, Truro; Trinity House Corporation; West Country Studies Library, Exeter.

And lastly, but by no means least, I would like to say a special thank you to the following: Tom Greeves for his unwavering interest and support throughout my research, and the helpful comments on the text, and Gerry Douglas-Sherwood of the Association of Lighthouse Keepers, who generously gave up his time to read through the completed text, made helpful suggestions and advised on the technical intricacies of lighthouses. Gerry and the Association also provided valuable information and images, for which I am very grateful. I would also like to thank Neil Jones, Trinity House Archivist, who provided and gave permission for the use of Trinity House plans and photographs that are used throughout the book.

PICTURE ACKNOWLEDGEMENTS
Association Lighthouse Keepers, Stan and Margret Butcher (Lighthouse Duo), Chance Bros, Robert Dorrien Smith, Gerry Douglas-Sherwood Sandra Gibson, Tom Greeves, Patricia Gumbrell, Greg Hopkins, Institution Civil Engineers, Sam Llewellyn, The National Archives, National Monuments Register, Christopher Nicholson, Jeremy Reseigh Watts and F. A. Webb, Royal Institution Cornwall, Neil Jones & Trinity House, Whittles Publishing, Peter Williams.

# BIBLIOGRAPHY

Adams, Francis & Pam *Star Castle & Its Garrison* Don Reynolds (2nd edn) n/d

Aldridge, Wendy *Hobnails and Seaboots* George G. Harrap & Co Ltd 1957 (reprint)

Anon, 'Mr William Tregarthen Douglass' in *Biographical Press Agency, The* February 1903

Austin, Keith *The Victorian Titanic – The loss of the S.S. Schiller in 1875* Halsgrove 2001

Bowley, R. L. *Scilly at War* Bowley Publications Ltd 2001

Boyle, Martin *Bishop Rock Lighthouse* B. & T. Publications 1997

Denton, Tony & Leach, Nicholas *Lighthouses of England and Wales – A complete guide* Landmark Publishing Ltd 2007

Douglas-Sherwood, Gerry *A Glossary of Lighthouse Service Terminology* Association of Lighthouse Keepers 2000

Douglass, William Tregarthen *The New Eddystone Lighthouse* The Institution of Civil Engineers 1883

Esquiros, Alphonse *Cornwall and its Coasts* Chapman and Hall 1865

Ferguson, John *Forged and Founded in Cornwall* Cornish Hillside Publications 2000

Forrester-Matthews, G. *The Isles of Scilly* George Ronald 1960

Gibson, Frank *Eye Witness 1958-1984* Privately published n/d

Gibson, Frank *Eye Witness A Continuation 1985-1990* Privately published n/d

Gibson, Frank *Eye Witness No. 3 1991-1997* Privately published n/d

Gill, Crispin *The Isles of Scilly* David & Charles 1975

Gillis, Richard *A Sea Miscellany of Cornwall and the Isles of Scilly* Harvey Barton 1968

Grigson, Geoffrey *The Scilly Isles* Gerald Duckworth & Co Ltd 1977 (reprinted from 1948)

Gumbrell, Patricia *Last of the Line* Whittles Publishing 2005

Hague, Douglas B. *Lighthouses of Wales – Their Architecture and Archaeology* Royal Commission on the Ancient and Historical Monuments of Wales 1994

Hall, Thomas *The T. W. Lawson – The Fate of the World's Only Seven Masted Schooner* The History Press 2006

Hunt, Robert & Rudler, F. W. *Ure's Dictionary of Arts, Manufactures and Mines* Longmans, Green & Co 1878

Inglis-Jones, Elisabeth *Augustus Smith of Scilly* Faber and Faber Ltd 1969

Jackson, Derrick *Lighthouses of England & Wales* David & Charles 1975

Jenkins, A. J. *Gigs and Cutters of the Isles of Scilly* Maggie Tucker (Reprint) 2002

Jenkins, Alf *The Scillonian and His Boat* Privately published 1982

Larn, Richard *Cornish Shipwrecks: The Isles of Scilly* David & Charles 1971

Larn, Richard *Ships, Shipwrecks and Maritime Incidents around the Isles of Scilly* Isles of Scilly Museum Publication No. 3 (Revised edn) 1999

Larn, Richard (Ed), *'Poor England has lost so many men'* The Council of the Isles of Scilly 2006

Lethbridge, Matt *All in a Lifetime* Privately Published 2003

Lethbridge, Richard *Behind the Eyebrows* Arden Craig Publications 1994

Lewis, W. J. *Ceaseless Vigil: My lonely years in the lighthouse service* George Harrap & Co Ltd 1970

Llewellyn, Sam *Emperor Smith The Man Who Built Scilly* The Dovecote Press 2005

*Lyonesse A Handbook for The Isles of Scilly* (4th edn) The Homeland Association Ltd 1906

McBride, Peter and Larn, Richard *Admiral Shovell's Treasure and Shipwreck in the Isles of Scilly* privately published 1999

Madden, Peter *Scilly's Building Heritage* Twelveheads Press 1996

Majdalany, Fred *The Red Rocks of Eddystone* White Lion Publishers 1974

Maybee, Robert *The Scillonian Poet* Isle of Scilly Museum Publication No.9 1973

Mudd, David *Cornwall & Scilly Peculiar* Bossiney Books 1979

Mumford, Clive *Portrait of the Isles of Scilly* Robert Hale & Co 1972

Nicholson, Christopher *Rock Lighthouses of Britain* Patrick Stephens 1983 and Whittles Publishing 2006

Noall, Cyril *Cornish Lights and Shipwrecks* D. Bradford Barton Ltd 1968

Noall, Cyril & Farr, Grahame *Wreck and Rescue Round the Cornish Coast II: The Story of the Land's End Lifeboats* D. Bradford Barton Ltd 1965

North, I. W. *A Week in the Isles of Scilly* E. Rowe, Penzance 1850

Padel, O. J. *Cornish Place-Names* Alison Hodge 1988

Parker, Tony *Lighthouse* Eland Publishing Ltd 2006

Pearson. Lynn F. *Lighthouses* Shire Publications Ltd 2003

*Report of the Commissioners appointed to enquire into the Condition and Management of Lights, Buoys, and Beacons 1861* Vols I & II. (Vol **XXV** 2793)

Sobel, Dava *Longitude* Fourth Estate, London 1996

Stanier, Peter *South West Granite – A History of the Granite Industry in Cornwall & Devon* Cornish Hillside Publications 1999

Sutton-Jones, Kenneth *To Safely Guide Their Way* B. & T. Publications 1998

Tarrant, Michael *Cornwall's Lighthouse Heritage* Twelveheads Press 2007

Tarrant, Michael *Trinity House – The Super Silent Service* Gomer Press 1998

Taylor, Harold *A Light at the Top* privately published CD n/d

Thomas, Charles *Exploration of a Drowned Landscape* B. T. Batsford Ltd, London 1985

Vyvyan, C. C. *The Scilly Isles* Robert Hale Ltd 1956

Ward, Edward 'My Month in a Lighthouse' *Picture Post* Hulton Press Ltd 1947

Watts, Jeremy Reseigh *Scilly Through the Eyes of The 'Duchess of Auriga'* Shepeard-Walwyn (Publishers) Ltd 2005

Whetter, Dr James *Cornwall in the 13th Century* Lyfrow Trelyspen 1998

Williams, Archibald *A Book of the Sea* Thomas Nelson & Sons Ltd n/d (c.1915?)

Williams, Thomas *Life of Sir James Nicholas Douglass FRS* Longmans Green & Co 1900

Woodman, R. & Wilson, J. *The Lighthouses of Trinity House* Thomas Reed Publications 2002


PERIODICALS ETC

*Cornish Telegraph, The* various

*Cornishman, The* various

*Daily Telegraph, The* 17.12.1990

*Flash* Trinity House, March 1993

*Guardian, The* March 31 1990

*Gentleman's Magazine, The* Jan-June 1850

*Illustrated London News*

*Kelly's Directory*, various

*Lamp*, various

*Minutes of the Proceedings of The Institution of Civil Engineers*, various

*Royal Cornwall Gazette*, various

*Scillonian, The* various

*South Devon and South Cornwall* Dulan & Co 1885

*Times, The* various

*Trewman's Exeter Flying Post*, various


**WEBSITES**

www.alk.co.uk

www.bbc.co.uk/cult/classic/bluepeter/lesleypetejohn/video/video10.shtml

www.cil.ie

www.divernet.com

www.genuki.org.uk/big/Lighthouses/Keepers.html

www.lawlor-pollock.com/llktrans-02.html

www.trinityhouse.co.uk

# INDEX